BUSINESS

AS

MISSION

BUSINESS
|AS|
MISSION

The Power of Business
in the Kingdom of God

MICHAEL R. BAER

YWAM
PUBLISHING
P.O. Box 55787 | Seattle, WA 98155

YWAM Publishing is the publishing ministry of Youth With A Mission. Youth With A Mission (YWAM) is an international missionary organization of Christians from many denominations dedicated to presenting Jesus Christ to this generation. To this end, YWAM has focused its efforts in three main areas: (1) training and equipping believers for their part in fulfilling the Great Commission (Matthew 28:19), (2) personal evangelism, and (3) mercy ministry (medical and relief work).

For a free catalog of books and materials, contact

YWAM Publishing
P.O. Box 55787, Seattle, WA 98155
(425) 771-1153 or (800) 922-2143
www.ywampublishing.com

Business as Mission: The Power of Business in the Kingdom of God
Copyright © 2006 by Michael R. Baer

10 09 08 07 06   10 9 8 7 6 5 4 3 2 1

Published by YWAM Publishing
P.O. Box 55787
Seattle, WA 98155

ISBN 1-57658-388-0

Library of Congress Cataloging-in-Publication Data

Baer, Michael R.
    Business as mission : the power of business in the kingdom of God
/ by Michael R. Baer.
    p. cm.
    ISBN-13: 978-1-57658-388-3
    ISBN-10: 1-57658-388-0
    1. Business—Religious aspects—Christianity. 2. Business ethics.
I. Title.
HF5388.B34 2006
261.8'5—dc22
                                                              2006022616

Printed in the United States of America

To Cindy, without whose lifelong support
none of what I care about would be possible.

ACKNOWLEDGEMENTS

Many people have had an impact on my pilgrimage and on the writing of this book. In typical fashion, I know I will forget someone, and I apologize in advance for that oversight. It is not intentional.

I want to thank my coworkers Gary C. and Tim W. for partnering with me in this endeavor of kingdom business, Lee Jacobs for the initial invitation to Central Asia where God began teaching me about business as mission, Pete S. whose friendship and missionary leadership was the anchor that launched all of this, and David B. who was there when this kingdom company started.

Marit Newton and Warren Walsh at YWAM Publishing have also been enormously helpful. This is my first book, and they believed in it and shepherded me through the process with grace and patience.

Finally, I want to give special acknowledgement to my wife, Cindy, for all her support and encouragement in this and all my projects in the Lord.

CONTENTS

PREFACE

*Businesspeople swamped me as I finished speaking to a busi-
ness group in Tampa. They were excited by the prospect that
they could use their business skills and their companies to serve
God. They had never been challenged like this before, but
they were rising to the call. As one of them said to me, "The
business community among Christians is like a vast reservoir
of resources just waiting to be tapped for world missions!"*

A great movement is beginning across North America and
around the world—the kingdom business or "business as mission" movement. I say this is a great movement not because it is large
but because I sense the hand of God in it and see a huge potential for
impacting the world for Christ.

Imagine what could happen if every Christian businessperson
recognized that God had a purpose for his or her company that was
greater than profit, employment, or customer satisfaction. Imagine if
the vast number of believing business owners and operators were to
turn their companies over to God to use for his glory. Imagine the
power and joy of integrating business and faith for God's kingdom.

Think of the financial, technological, and human resources that would come into play. Think of the ways in which entire societies could be transformed for Christ.

We who are serious about our faith and our walk before God spend a great amount of time in our businesses; in fact, we spend more time on our corporate pursuits than on any other single part of our lives! Do we want that time to be wasted and underutilized, or do we want to discover how to make that time fully honor the Lord? The purpose of this book is to explore how companies can align with God's purpose and bring him glory.

My own story reflects this journey.

After coming to Christ in college, I spent the first fourteen years of my adult life in the pastoral ministry—youth work, planting two churches, serving a third, and launching a Christian school. The Lord blessed my ministry, and I can truthfully say I enjoyed it and was secure in my call to it. However, over time I began to sense God leading me into a different area. I began to desire to minister "free of charge" and to be out in the business world with lost people. I especially wanted to get away from the constant discounting of the gospel that occurred because people I witnessed to believed that sharing the gospel was my job.

In the early 1980s I began to dabble in business while still in the pastorate. I was testing the waters, so to speak, and seeking to know what God might want me to do. Eventually I left the formal pastorate and spent the next ten years in business—starting several companies (including the one I now own) and leading turnaround endeavors in corporations owned by others. God was pleased to use me in both the pastorate and the corporate world, and I thank him for it. Opportunities abounded to communicate the gospel and to encourage believers I met along the way. It was an exciting time. It was always fun to share how God had led me into the pastorate and then into business—these two apparently distinct parts of my life.

However, just as I sensed a leading from God out of the formal pastorate and into business, I also began to sense that there had to be more in my business life than just being a Christian witness on the job.

I began to pray and ask God to show me how these two apparently distinct parts of my life could actually come together—fourteen years in ministry and ten years in business. Were they separate chapters, or were they, in fact, parts of a greater whole, the "big picture" that God had in store for me?

The answer to my questions came in the strangest of places. In 1993 I was invited to travel to a Muslim area of the former Soviet Union to develop and deliver leadership and management training for medical students. While there, I had what I have come to call the "for this was I born" experience. I finally understood why God had given me seminary training and pastoral experience as well as passion and success in business. His plan was to bring both together in my service for him. Specifically, he desired to use me through business to minister to those I could never reach otherwise. Through my work of business training, relationship and witness opportunities opened that I could never have imagined. God began to bless my work in powerful ways. For the next four years I returned to the former Soviet Union annually with teams of volunteer Christian business leaders to give business seminars and share the gospel with those who attended.

Even with God's blessing on the volunteer work, I still sensed that the picture was not yet complete. Then, in 1997, I was approached by missionaries working in the same part of the world and asked to develop a program whereby impoverished and disenfranchised Christians could learn to start their own businesses. Their idea was that these persecuted believers could escape unemployment (over 90 percent in the Christian community in one country), provide for their families, support their local church, and even use their new businesses as a basis of church planting in remote areas. We launched this new program in 1998, and today the work that came out of that meeting is operating in more than twenty locations around the world, helping persecuted Christian minorities start businesses to provide economic traction for their own indigenous church-planting movements. At the same time, I left the company I had been working for and started a new consulting company, my current company, for the sole purpose of providing flexible employment for those who wanted to be a part of business missions overseas while remaining involved in business at home.[1]

Today, a strong, for-profit consulting firm and an international microbusiness development agency exist as the result. Staff members and associates who share a commitment to Christ and to kingdom business work together along with hundreds of volunteers from other companies to take their business expertise and align it with church-planting ministries among the unreached.

What I have come to learn through all of this is that there are no "parts" to my life. My story may represent different chapters, but they are all part of one book, a book with one unified story, being written by God. I no longer wonder why God led me out of the pastorate and into business. I no longer think of it as leaving the ministry. Instead, I have begun to see that in God's kingdom all things are equally sanctified by him and unified in him. For Christian business leaders, this leads to what I call "the seamless integration of business and mission." To pursue this seamless integration, we must reject the unbiblical thinking that our lives can be compartmentalized into the sacred and secular or that business and ministry are by definition separate activities. Scripture teaches us rather to embrace the truth that all of Christ's servants have callings that are high and holy and equally pleasing to the Lord. If God has called us into business, our goal is to discover why and to act on that purpose. As we do so, God's creation will be blessed, and he will be glorified.

I certainly don't expect that everyone will agree with what I have to say. I am, to quote my wife, "often wrong but never silent." I only hope to stir up thinking and to promote greater dialogue on these critical issues among those who find themselves called by God into the ministry of business.

---

1. Because of the sensitive areas in which we work, the names of the company, ministry, and countries in which we work will not be used in this book.

MY COMPANY: CHRISTIAN BUSINESS OR KINGDOM BUSINESS?

As we sat around the outdoor table, I was encouraged to see business owners willing to spend the weekend learning about kingdom business. I asked them to determine whether their businesses were secular, Christian, or kingdom businesses. Our conversation grew lively, and I could tell that they were deeply interested in answering the question. I find that business owners all over the United States and Great Britain match their eagerness, and I am hearing about similar conversations in all developed countries. Business owners are awakening to the potential of building a kingdom business.

Over the past ten years, much has been written on the subject of the Christian in business and about Christian business. More recently a few articles and books have emerged on the topic of "kingdom business." Are these the same thing described by different names, or are they in fact different? I believe that they are distinctly different and that our understanding of that difference is critical to our ability to make our professional lives count fully for the Lord.

The term *Christian business* is commonly used to refer to either a business that is owned by a Christian or a business managed according to Christian principles. Sometimes it is used to describe a company that is actually involved in some kind of religious work, such as a Christian music company or a Christian bookstore. On the other hand, when I speak of a *kingdom business* or *kingdom company,* I use the term to describe a business that is specifically, consciously, clearly, and intentionally connected to the establishment of Christ's kingdom in this world. In other words, it is directly involved in making disciples of all nations—beginning at home but with international involvement too.[1]

To some this may seem like splitting hairs. On one level, I would agree. The reason I would agree is that any business that is *truly* managed by biblical principles will *necessarily be connected* to what God is doing in the world, for example, discipling the nations. In his last conversations with his followers on earth, which we know as the Great Commission, Jesus made his purpose very clear. "Teach people, all people, to follow me," he said in essence (see Matt. 28:18–20). I remember speaking at a church missions conference a few years ago. My daughter asked me afterward, "How can people call themselves disciples of Christ and not be obedient to the Great Commission? Isn't that a central part of what Jesus told us to do?" She was right, of course, and what she said applies to Christian business as well. If we are committed to running our companies according to what Jesus said, we must be committed to connecting our companies to the Great Commission!

Yet it is precisely this logic that leads me to split this hair. A great breakdown occurs at this point that must be corrected. "Yes," says the Christian business leader, "I am deeply committed to the Great Commission. In fact, I am working hard to get more time away from my Christian business so I can do more Great Commission work." As admirable as this may seem, it falls far short of what God has in

---

1. There is another, related movement in the U.S. often referred to as "marketplace ministry." The thrust of the teaching in marketplace ministry is primarily an encouragement to Christians in business (owners and employees) to be more open and effective in sharing the gospel with their coworkers. I applaud this greatly and thoroughly support it. However, it is still not the same as kingdom business, at least as I'm using the term. To be a kingdom business there must be intentional connection to God's eternal purposes in the world, a connection that will ultimately lead in some way to involvement in world missions.

mind. God is not so much interested in your taking time *off work* to "do ministry" as he is in teaching you how to use the time you are *at work* to serve him and his purposes—which may very well be your true ministry. It is not only connecting our nonworking lives to the Great Commission that pleases God; he wants us to connect our businesses to his plan as well. This connection defines a true kingdom company as opposed to a merely Christian company.

The core of this entire book centers on one simple but profoundly vital question: Is my business a Christian business or a kingdom business?

There are four characteristics of a kingdom business. These four characteristics form the outline of this book. As we examine them together, let us use them as a standard to help us set our businesses apart. Here are the characteristics:

- A kingdom business is *vocational*; that is, it is something to which God has called us.
- A kingdom business is *intentional*; that is, God has a very specific purpose for each business as we discover and commit to it.
- A kingdom business is *relational*; that is, in business God blesses us with a huge set of relationships we would never have otherwise. We value these people as God does.
- A kingdom business is *operational*; that is, the way in which we operate our businesses impacts and reflects upon the kingdom.

The following overview summarizes the major thrust of each of the four sections of the book.

Vocational: Business Is a Calling from God

For centuries, in varying degrees, the church has held to a clear division between clergy and laity and between sacred and secular. We have thought in terms of those who have a holy calling from God to serve in "full-time" ministry and those who essentially are not called to anything special. For generations, the laity has worked in the *secular* marketplace and on the farm in order to generate income to live and to support the *sacred* work of the clergy. Despite constant teaching on the duty of the everyday Christian and the priesthood of all believers, the divide between the "called" and the "uncalled" has continued to grow. And it is very much with us today.

Ask serious Christians about their calling and you will probably hear words about serving in the church. Dig deeper and you'll quickly discover the sense that even though they seek to serve God in some way (usually related to church work), businesspeople often feel inadequate or substandard. "If I were really faithful," they confess, "God would call me into the ministry." Ministry calling and business are seen as separate. I have often heard people in ministry refer to being called out of business into "ministry" so that they could serve the Lord. One missionary actually told me he had been "delivered" from business.

Those in full-time Christian service recognize the need for funding and are clear that not everyone can be called to public ministry. But sadly, many don't recognize that all their brothers and sisters in Christ, including those in business, are just as called as they are. They may minister *to* the business community. They draw funding *from* the business community. They encourage service by leaders in the business community—but this service is separate from their everyday work and usually in the context of church. All of this subtly confirms what businesspeople have come to believe: that at best business is a necessary evil that God somehow redeems through giving.

The simple truth from the Bible is far different from the conventional wisdom of the day. In God's kingdom, business, like every aspect of life, is under the call of God and therefore can be a calling in itself. Christ is not merely Lord of the church; he has laid his claim of authority and kingship on business, on family, on government, on all of life (see Col. 1:16–20). To recognize the lordship of Christ *over* business is the first step toward recognizing his call on your life *to* business.

In Ephesians 4:1, Paul urges believers to "live a life worthy of the calling [the vocation] you have received." Applied correctly, this verse speaks to all believers—not just ministers and missionaries—and tells them that God has called them all. God has not called some and left others uncalled. He has not set up a distinction between clergy and laity, nor does he recognize a difference between those who serve in full-time Christian service and those who serve as full-time Christians in business. We are all called. We are all designated as those belonging to Christ, those who walk with Christ, and those whose lives are to be lived under the call.

Not only do we not see a distinction between the called and the uncalled in Scripture, we also do not see a distinction between those called to something high and holy and those called to something that is a necessary evil. We see that all are called and all are called to something high and holy. This is exactly what Paul says when he writes to the Christians in Rome as those "called to be saints" (Rom. 1:7). The literal translation is that they were called to be holy or holy ones, called to be sacred. In other words, whatever God has called you to do and be is exactly what he desired from the beginning of time, and it is, by definition, perfect and holy (see Rom. 12:1–2).

What this means is that if I am a businessperson, this may well be my calling from God and, if so, I should look no further. I should not fall victim to thinking that my activities in sales or management or employment or any other facet of business are a noncall or a less-than call. I should view my life in its entirety as a high calling from God, and I should view my business as a part of that holy invitation. I should rejoice in the fact that God called me and that since he called me, he has a purpose for putting me exactly where I am.

Intentional: God Has a Unique Purpose for Each Business

Once we have begun to recognize that we are not substandard Christians or less-than-called persons, once we have begun to operate in the full understanding that business is our calling from God, we are ready to begin exploring the next question: What is the specific purpose that God has in mind for my business? The calling of Ephesians 4:1 is a general calling to live a life worthy of God's grace. However, in another part of Ephesians, Paul tells us that there is more than a general calling on the Christian's life; there is a specific calling, a specific purpose, something that God intended to come out of that life.

In Ephesians 2:10, Paul tells us that we are "created in Christ Jesus to do good works, which *God prepared in advance* for us to do" (emphasis added). The implications of this verse are manifold. First, it tells us that God has a plan that he developed long before we ever came into being. Second, it tells us that he intends for us to walk in that plan, to fulfill it by doing the good works he planned for us to do. In other words, we are called *generally* (which confirms the high and holy nature of whatever we are engaged in) and we are called *specifically* to fulfill God's plan for our lives (which defines our personal purpose). Since some of us are called to business, it follows that we are called to some purpose for that business. Furthermore, if there is a plan and if we are to fulfill it, we should put great effort into discovering exactly what that plan is and connecting our lives and our businesses to it. We'll explore this more fully in chapters 3 and 4.

If this is true—that God has a unique plan for my life and my business—it is vital that I discover and execute that plan. It is vital that I am very intentional about my business. Why? Because I recognize that God has a purpose for it!

In working with disenfranchised believers in unreached[2] areas as I described in the preface, one thing we emphasize with them is the need to identify and articulate the "kingdom purpose" of their business. We want to start them early in their business careers recognizing that their business is not their own but something given to them by God and that there is nothing higher than fulfilling the purpose for which it was given. I am constantly amazed at the visionary and expansive thinking that many of our students use to arrive at their own unique kingdom-purpose statement.

What about your business? Do you know what its purpose is? Can you articulate why God called it into being and called you to lead it? And if you know this purpose, are you implementing it?

Some of the more obvious purposes for which I have seen God create businesses are to fund church and missions activity, to generate

---

2. Missiologists debate the exact meaning of *unreached*. For the purpose of this book, the term refers to those people groups who are least reached with the gospel, usually measured by less than 2 percent of the population being evangelical and there being no self-sustaining Christian presence.

profit that can be given to those in need, to provide employment for the unemployed, and to establish relationships (with employees, vendors, and customers) through which the gospel can be communicated and demonstrated. Less obvious purposes may include opening political dialogue with leaders at home and abroad, enabling Christ-centered relief work in war-torn areas of the world, challenging traditional concepts of missions, and starting new kingdom companies around the world. This is by no means an exhaustive list. The important point is to recognize that God has a purpose—a kingdom purpose—for your business. He called you to business, to a specific business, and he planned before time began to use it for his glory. Do you know that plan?

On a recent trip to Indonesia I was meeting with a young Christian business owner. She and her brother operated a furniture factory on one of the larger islands of that predominantly Muslim country. She asked me to help her identify her kingdom purpose. I asked her about her employees—who they were and where they came from. She told me that they were all from a particular tribe, which just happens to be the most unreached tribe in all of Indonesia. I told her to look no further. God had handed her a personal mission field inside the four walls of her business.

Relational: Relationships Are Where Christ Is Glorified

The two greatest commandments, according to Jesus, are to "love the Lord your God with all your heart and with all your soul and with all your mind and with all your strength" and to "love your neighbor as yourself" (Mark 12:30–31). Clearly, the Lord is telling us that relationships are primary in his kingdom—relationship with God and relationships with one another. And what better place to build relationships with one another than in and through business?

Business is not only factories, computers, offices, balance sheets, and sales materials. Business is also relationships: employees, shareholders, vendors, customers, competitors, and government officials. These relationships, without which business cannot exist, are the areas Jesus wants us to focus on. What a gift! God has called us with a specific purpose and then placed us into a set of relationships that he calls primary. What an opportunity! We meet people in our daily activities who will never attend a church or a neighborhood Bible study. Some are disillusioned or fallen believers who question the very relevance of God to their lives. Others are obstinate rejecters of the gospel and avowed enemies of the Cross who see nothing of value in the visible marks of the Christian religion. Some are seekers who have a genuine interest in Christ but an uninformed understanding of true Christianity. Others are just ignorant, never having seen or heard any credible representation of the good news. Whatever the case, God has placed us in these relationships with these people only through the medium of business, and it is his intent that we reach out to them in his name.

When we transport our business overseas into a non-Christian culture, all of these factors are multiplied. A good friend of mine describes the Asian culture in which he lives and works as a collection of relational networks. These networks are almost impossible to break into unless you find the one person who is the "gatekeeper." A relationship with this gatekeeper ultimately gives access to dozens and perhaps hundreds of people who need the gospel. In his case, the way of finding the gatekeeper comes through his business relationships. It is through his factory that this network is explored.

We cannot read the Bible without seeing how important relationships are to God. We cannot read the Bible without encountering numerous commands that are explanations of what loving your neighbor looks like in real life. Love them. Serve them. Deal justly with them. Forgive them. Hold them accountable. Encourage them. Share Christ with them. Teach them. Learn from them. Honor them. Live at peace with them. Recognize their authority. The list goes on and on.

Why is this so important? Because it is not the words or the actions of the visible church that impact people for Christ as much as it is our lives, our attitudes, and our behavior lived out in our everyday existence. Whether they know we are Christians or not, people are touched by us in the context of relationship. And through a vast number of touches, they are influenced toward God or away from him. Therefore, a kingdom business places great emphasis on how it relates to people and is constantly taking stock of relationships—measuring them by Scripture.

Several years ago, I was asked to serve on the board of founders of a university in one of the new Central Asian republics. One of my interests as a new board member was in providing scholarships to deserving students through my business. The president of the university, a Muslim, asked me why I would do this kindness to her students and wanted to know whether I was a Christian. I answered that I was, and to my surprise, she smiled and said, "I knew it!"

Operational: A Kingdom Business Is Managed with Excellence

What about the basic operation of our businesses? Does God speak about that? Does that have a kingdom application? Yes! It is not enough to know the high calling of God on our lives. It is not enough to have discovered and begun implementation of God's unique purpose for our businesses. It is not enough to simply seek to live before people in a way that honors God. We must also strive to operate our businesses in every facet in such a way that God is pleased and glorified. Consider the words of 1 Corinthians 10:31: "So whether you eat or drink or whatever you do, do it all for the glory of God."

It matters how we operate our business. We are called to operate it with excellence, to use the best practices, to create a great company, to so live that the daily functions of business also testify to the presence of God in our midst.

On a practical level this means that there is no Christian excuse for sloppy business habits. There is no "I was doing ministry" explanation for not running an excellent company. On the contrary, if God has called us to this endeavor, then the running of our business should reflect that. Our sales processes should be honorable and effective. Our financial management must be honest and aggressive. Our profit performance should be outstanding. Our technology should be cutting edge. Our employment practices should be exemplary.

Our vendor-payment records should be timely and accurate. Our collections should be filled with accountability. Our customer service should reflect the servant heart of Christ. Our employee development should be the stuff about which books are written. In other words, if bestselling author Tom Peters were to go on another "search for excellence," he should arrive at our doors.

The size to which God intends to allow our businesses to grow may differ, but the standard by which we are to operate is the same. It is high. It is world class—no, it is heavenly class. In the Old Testament, God was very clear about the sacrifices that were acceptable to him; they were to be perfect, free from blemish, and not second-rate. The same principle should guide our attitudes in the operation of our businesses. Our conduct of business is our offering to him. Therefore, it should be given with an eye to perfection.

How often have we seen a fish symbol on the car that just cut us off in traffic? What is our reaction? And how often have we seen a similar outward expression of faith betrayed in business by shoddy practices or even underhanded dealings? Indeed, how well I remember a member of my church telling me that he would never do business with another Christian. When I asked why, he explained that he expected to be taken advantage of by unbelievers and kept his guard up; when dealing with brothers and sisters in Christ, he lowered his guard and ended up being cheated.

A kingdom business is operated well. It is run by kingdom principles and according to kingdom standards.

Conclusion

So we see that there are four traits of a true kingdom business: a high and holy calling, a discovered and executed purpose, a valued set of vital relationships, and a demand for operational excellence. These are high standards. They are mile markers along the journey. We are all in process. But this is our destination.

May God bless us and grant us the grace to encourage each other along the way. Sola Dei Gloria!

1

A KINGDOM BUSINESS IS
VOCATIONAL

1

BUSINESS IS A GOOD THING FROM GOD

I was not prepared the first time I heard the challenge. The Central Asian pastor stood in the conference and politely but firmly asked, "How can a Christian be involved in business? It's totally corrupt and of the world." Since then, I've heard that question in one form or another dozens of times and in dozens of countries. The belief that business is inherently evil appears to be a worldwide tenet of the faith.

In much of the world there is a fundamental conviction among sincere Christians that there is something intrinsically wrong with business and that no serious follower of Christ would go into business, much less consider it a calling. In the former Soviet republics, the shadow of Marxist–Leninism can still be felt in this regard; indeed, one of the most serious crimes against the Soviet state was profiteering or speculation. Buddhist- and Hindu-background believers feel a similar distrust of business as if it will stain the soul. And even in America and Western Europe, it is not uncommon to hear or read of Christian leaders with a negative view of the business world.

If we are going to explore the concept of kingdom business, our misunderstanding of the nature of business is a major hurdle we are going to have to overcome. A kingdom business begins with the premise that it is a calling from God and that business leadership is something that is the perfect will of God. Until a believer accepts that God has called him or her into business, it will be impossible to really embrace the concept of kingdom business. The next chapter will deal more fully with the high and holy nature of that call; first, however, I need to address the more basic question of the legitimacy of business.

What Is Wrong with Business?

To be sure, there is much that is wrong in the business world. Greed, dishonesty, envy, extravagance, exploitation, sweatshops, and environmental pollution are just some of the things we see in the business world that alarm all moral persons, including committed Christians.

When I ask individuals or groups of people what they think about business, I hear things like Bhopal (site of the Union Carbide poison leak that killed so many Indians), the *Exxon Valdez* (an oil tanker that ran aground and ruptured in Alaskan waters with devastating ecological impact), and Donald Trump (the most common example of conspicuous consumption). I hear about tax evasion, layoffs that occur simultaneously with massive executive bonuses, pharmaceutical giants marketing products later proven to be unsafe or even life threatening, and the growing gap between the haves and the have-nots. I hear about child labor abuses in Central America and the excessive parties paid for with company money by Tyco executives.

There is no question that things are seriously amiss in the world of business and enterprise. But are the things we see as wrong a reason to condemn business itself? The answer is foundational to any hope of a Christian finding his or her way in business.

Business is not wrong or evil any more than the family or government is evil by nature. Let me repeat that: business is not evil. The problem with business, just as with everything else in creation, is not in the institution itself but in the *people of the institution.* Business is not corrupt; the human heart is corrupt. Business is not greedy; the human heart is greedy. Business is not self-centered; the human heart is self-centered. Jeremiah put it this way when he said, "The heart is deceitful above all things and beyond cure. Who can understand it?" (Jer. 17:9). The fact that wicked people do wicked things in business does not make business itself wicked.

In one of my favorite movies, *Driving Miss Daisy,* the aging Miss Daisy, played by Jessica Tandy, wrecks her car. Subsequently, her insurance is cancelled and she is unable to drive. Arguing with her son, she insists that it wasn't her fault. "I can't help it if the car misbehaved," she says. To which her son replies, "Mama, cars do not behave. They are behaved upon." In the same way, a business does not behave. It is behaved upon—often by self-centered people; consequently, we see self-centered results.

Who would argue that the family unit is evil based on some of the horrible dysfunction we see in families around us today? Or who would say that all government is evil based on a murderous former dictator like Saddam Hussein? Who would argue that all sports are evil because some athletes cheat or take steroids? How about the church—would we determine all churches to be corrupt because a particular priest is guilty of child abuse? In each of these areas we would conclude that the institution is a good one intended by God for good purposes. People, not the institution, are the problem.

Business Is a Good Thing from God

When I first started working overseas and helping impoverished Christians start their own businesses, I was immediately faced with opposition. I very quickly had to research and come up with a biblical explanation for the legitimacy of business and enterprise or my ministry either would cease to be relevant or, worse, would drive a wedge between pastors who believed business was evil and my students who desperately needed business to survive. What came out of that study was a one-day session with which we still start all training and to which we invite the pastors of all our students. We call this session "Business Is a Good Thing from God." Whether we lead a business in the West or in the developing world, understanding the legitimacy of business from Scripture is essential to pursuing a kingdom company.

Business and Enterprise Are a Part of Creation

The very first thing to understand about the legitimacy of business is that business was a part of God's creation prior to the Fall. Now clearly I don't mean that God created companies, factories, office buildings, or stores in the Garden of Eden. What I do mean is that a mechanism for wealth creation, time use, managing the environment, and meeting physical needs was set in place from the beginning. That mechanism is business (or enterprise). The very word *business* derives from the concept of "busy-ness," meaning that which keeps us productively occupied (hence occupation), or busy. What kept Adam and Eve occupied, among other things, was their tending of the garden—the very activity that God sanctified and through which he intended to provide for their physical (and other) needs. Since then business has taken many forms, but the fundamental function of wealth creation has always been in place. It is a part of God's original creation and the way he intended his creation to work.

There is a great sense of completeness when we think of creation this way. When God made the world, he set up an institution for populating the earth and reproducing humanity—the family. He set up a mechanism for overseeing relationships between human beings and, later, the nations that would come from them—government. He also set up a mechanism for worship—the church. The fact that in the beginning the family had only two members, the government had a King (God himself) and only two subjects, and the church, the believing and worshiping people of God, had only two adherents does not make these institutions less valid. Why, then, should it be any different when we consider the original business—God's first mechanism for providing for human needs—which consisted of only two workers and two customers?

Let's dig a little deeper into what God created humanity to do. Look at the record in Genesis 1:26–31:

> Then God said, "Let us make man in our image, in our likeness, and let them rule over the fish of the sea and the birds

of the air, over the livestock, over all the earth, and over all the creatures that move along the ground." So God created man in his own image, in the image of God he created him; male and female he created them.

God blessed them and said to them, "Be fruitful and increase in number; fill the earth and subdue it. Rule over the fish of the sea and the birds of the air and over every living creature that moves on the ground."

Then God said, "I give you every seed-bearing plant on the face of the whole earth and every tree that has fruit with seed in it. They will be yours for food. And to all the beasts of the earth and all the birds of the air and all the creatures that move on the ground—everything that has the breath of life in it—I give every green plant for food." And it was so.

God saw all that he had made, and it was very good. And there was evening, and there was morning—the sixth day.

This passage provides a foundational theology of work and business. First, note that it started with God (v. 26). Second, it involved what has come to be called the "creation mandate" in which God entrusts creation to Adam and Eve and instructs them to manage it on his behalf—"subdue it." Many theologians see in this that God intended us to explore and make use of the various minerals and potential within creation yet without destruction. Third, humanity's mastery over creation included all plants "for food." And fourth, this arrangement was "very good" (v. 31). What we see here is clear: God's plan included setting up a working enterprise (in this case a farming business and an environmental exploration and management firm) through which humanity's needs would be met. In other words, the original couple were in business; the business was very small and the market was tiny, but it was real. And it was all *before the Fall!*

Once, while I was teaching on this subject in Mongolia, a pastor challenged me and asked about the difference between working and being in business. Work, labor, sweat, physical effort, and employment—all these things seemed honorable or at least necessary to him. However, being in business, owning a business, employing others, and exercising commerce, so it seemed to him were dishonorable and exploitative. I was able to show him that unless we choose to believe that God's will was that we all live as subsistence farmers, an idea not supported by the Genesis text or any other, we will see that sooner or later individual labor would become business. Production of food, animal husbandry, distribution of food, building shelter, mining the earth, manufacturing goods, buying and selling goods, and banking would spill over the bounds of the original family, and commerce between individuals, families, villages, tribes, and countries would inevitably come into being *apart from the Fall*. This is exactly what business is! What God set in motion in creation was intended to grow and expand; it has continued to do so, as have the family, the church as the people of God, and every other institution he set up.

Businesspeople in Scripture

When Adam and Eve sinned and corruption entered the world (see Gen. 3), that corruption impacted all that God had made, including business. That is why we see so many things wrong in the business world just as we do in the rest of the world. Yet God never condemned business or those in business. Business was and is still part of his creation plan, and Scripture is filled with examples of those who were in business and used by God.

Consider Lydia, the first convert to Christ in Europe. What was her profession? She was a merchant, a "dealer in purple cloth" (Acts 16:14). Essentially, Lydia was a business owner who either produced and sold or procured and sold a fine fabric that was in demand in her day. While her career is not specifically praised, it is certainly not criticized.

What was the profession of Peter, James, and John? These men were in business as fishermen. No doubt someone reading this will say that they left all that to follow Christ. It is certainly true that they left all to become Jesus' disciples, but there is no evidence that they ceased to ply their trade on occasion, nor is there any implication that they left their business because it was wrong. In fact, after their time with Christ and in preparation for their ministries, they continued to fish (see John 21).

Philemon, to whom the epistle is addressed by Paul, was obviously in some kind of business. This is not explicit in the text, but it is certainly reasonable to assume that this wealthy Christian had come to his fortune through some kind of business enterprise. He had certainly learned how to put his wealth to good use, supporting ministry, refreshing the saints, and letting the local church congregate in his home. Read the short letter for yourself. Is there any hint of negativism in Paul toward Philemon's occupation?

What about Amos and David? They were shepherds. What about Luke? He was a physician. What about all of the skilled craftsmen of the Old Testament who were used of God to build and decorate the tabernacle and, later, the temple? Consider Jethro (see Exodus 18), Moses' father-in-law; he was a shepherd (and some would argue the original management consultant) whose advice to Moses facilitated the orderly leading of the Israelite throng. And what did Abraham, the father of the faithful, do for a living? Among other things he was a major farmer, herder, and employer. The judges, like Deborah and Gideon, who ruled Israel before the time of King Saul, were often bivocational, meaning they held office in the government and operated some form of business venture at the same time. These and many more examples could be cited. Each is an example of a faithful servant of God involved in a trade or business. There is no hint that God had a problem with their vocations.

Before we leave this point, I want to look at two more examples: Paul and Jesus. The very term *tentmaker* is derived from Paul's business background (Acts 18:3), and his skill in this area is something Paul used to enhance his ministry, to network with others, and to provide his physical needs while serving churches free of charge (see 1 Cor. 9:6–18). And even our Lord himself was directly involved in the family business of carpentry. He, his father, and his earthly brothers made furniture or doors or wooden tools and then sold their products to provide for the family. Surely no one would consider that Jesus participated in something inherently corrupt.

God's Uses for Business in Scripture

So why did God create business in the first place? What is his purpose? In Scripture, we can find two major reasons for business: provision, as we have already seen, and relationship.

In terms of provision, business is God's primary means to provide for people. There are exceptions, of course—Elijah being fed by ravens and Israel gathering manna are examples—but for the most part, God's clear intention is for us to work, to farm, to do business in order to earn the bread we eat (see 2 Thess. 3:12). Not only do we work to provide for ourselves and our families, but we also do business to provide for the poor among us (see Eph. 4:28)—people about whom God cares very much. And finally, God uses enterprise to enable us to give to his work and to his church (see Prov. 3:9–10, Mal. 3:10–12, 1 Cor. 16:1–2).

Can God provide for us without business? Of course he can and often does. Nevertheless, for reasons not revealed, he has chosen to grant us what we need to live through the means of our work and enterprise, through business.

Business has another key use in Scripture: it is a means of relating to the world around us and, in those relationships, demonstrating the grace of God in our lives. Paul, for example, met and ministered to Aquila and Priscilla through work (see Acts 18:1–3). Think, in your own life, how many people you have met through your job or through your company whom you would never have met otherwise. In our overseas work there are countless examples of people coming to Christ, indeed of entire churches being planted, through relationships first formed in business endeavors. In fact, one of our graduates in Central Asia is on his third business start-up, and through the relationships that came through business, he has planted over twenty house churches in a region where previously there were none!

Conclusion

We can see from Scripture that God established business as part of his good creation before the Fall. The corruption of sin has affected business, just as evil has touched all of life and all of God's creation.

Even so, God used businesspeople throughout biblical history and continues to use business in our lives today. Business is a good thing from God.

2

THE HIGH CALLING FROM
GOD IN BUSINESS

*"I can't wait to retire," my friend told me. "Then I can give
my time to ministry." I can't tell you how many times I've
heard this kind of statement from committed disciples of
Christ. God is using these people in their businesses, yet their
view of serving Christ requires them to think in terms of
retirement from business and entry into "the ministry."*

T he kind of thinking expressed by my friend is common and
contributes to a major problem among Christian business owners as well as the rest of the Christian world. Essentially, our culture
holds to a standard that we are living in a world where some do the
sacred work that matters to God while others do the secular (the
word comes from the Latin term for "worldly") work, where some are
called by God to ministry while the rest of us labor as the uncalled to
support them. Nothing could be further from the truth!

God's Call Unites Life

In the 1981 Best Picture Oscar winner *Chariots of Fire*, there is a powerful scene in which missionary-athlete Eric Liddell tries to explain
his sense of calling to his sister Jennie. Liddell says, "I believe God

made me for a purpose—for China." Had he stopped there, most of us would have clearly understood his statement—he had surrendered to the high and holy calling of missions. That's clearly how Jennie understood him. But Liddell continued. "But he also made me fast. And when I run, I feel his pleasure.... To win is to honor him." He then went on to win a gold medal at the 1924 Olympics in Paris, to serve God in China, and to inspire generations of young people to follow the Savior.

Eric Liddell's statement about being fast and honoring God through running is hard for most modern Christians to understand. It was hard for Liddell's sister to understand. Athletics, like business, seems to be on the downside of the great divide between vocations that God uses and those he, at best, tolerates. Had Liddell's comparison been to teaching, medicine, charity work, or humanitarian relief, we would have had no real struggle. But how can God "make him" for athletics? Or, as in my case, how can God "make me" for business?

I like to rewrite the script of *Chariots of Fire* in my mind so that it reads like this:

> ERIC: Jennie, I know God wants me to serve him overseas.
> JENNIE: Great! I've prayed that would happen.
> ERIC: But, Jennie, God also made me a great salesman. And when I close a deal, I feel his pleasure.
> JENNIE: What?!
> ERIC: Yes. He made me a salesman, and to sell is to honor him.

Does that exchange sound funny? To most of us it sounds ridiculous. Maybe business is a good thing from God—but to be made for it? To feel his pleasure when we do it? To succeed in business is to honor him? Some would say that's taking it a bit far.

The reason that an exchange like this sounds so strange is that all of us are the product of generations of Christianity that were built on what has become known as the "sacred-secular dichotomy." It is my deep conviction that nothing has disabled the church of Jesus Christ in its ministry to the world more than this false system that breaks life into compartments—sacred or secular, holy or profane, part of God's call or not part of God's call.

In the beginning it was not this way. It is clear from the teachings of Jesus and the apostles that all of life is sacred to God. Christ's kingdom affects all things, even things as mundane as eating and drinking; Let's look again at Paul's encouragement in 1 Corinthians 10:31—"So whether you eat or drink or whatever you do, *do it all for the glory of God*" (emphasis added). In other words, you can feel God's pleasure and honor him, as Eric Liddell did, in every legitimate activity of life—in running, in teaching, in preaching, and in doing business. Dallas Willard writes:

> There is truly no division between sacred and secular except what we have created. And that is why the division of the legitimate roles and functions of human life into the sacred and secular does incalculable damage to our individual lives and to the cause of Christ. Holy people must stop going into "church work" as their natural course of action and take up holy orders in farming, industry, law, education, banking, and journalism with the same zeal previously given to evangelism or to pastoral and missionary work.[1]

All of life is sacred for the Christian, and the realization of that truth sets us free to serve God in all aspects of our existence.

I was having coffee one afternoon with one of my associates, a new member of our consulting firm. Bill was struggling with the concept of sales and business development. He just couldn't bring himself to feel good about it. I asked him, "When is a bird most honoring to God, when it is flying and singing or when it is preaching? Bill laughed and answered, "Obviously when it's flying and singing." "The reason for that," I explained, "is that the bird is honoring God the most when it is doing exactly what God made it to do. Right?" He

---

1. Dallas Willard, *The Spirit of the Disciplines: Understanding How God Changes Lives* (New York: Harper Collins, 1991), 214.

agreed, and then I asked him, "Which activity glorifies God more for a human—sharing the gospel or selling a product?" Bill smiled. "That's easy. Sharing the gospel." My response shocked him. "Wrong," I said. "What glorifies God is not the quality of the activity but whether it is what he wants me to do at that moment." In other words, what honors God is bound up not in the activity itself but, like the bird, in doing what we were made to do, in following his call on our lives.

It is in understanding and embracing the call of God on our lives that we escape the prison of the sacred-secular split and enter into the freedom of life in Christ's kingdom. What were we made for? A bird was made to fly; a fish was made to swim. What were you made for? The answer is your calling.

Every Christian Has a Calling

The first thing we have to do is cast off the false belief that the term *call* refers only to professional ministers like missionaries, pastors, or seminary professors. "I was called to preach," says one. "I was called to ministry," says another. "I was called to the mission field," say some.

In point of fact, all Christians are called. Consider the following survey of verses from the New Testament.

"To all in Rome who are loved by God and called to be saints:" (Rom. 1:7). This verse alone is enough to debunk the idea that only some believers are called. Indeed, the Greek reads, "to all who are in Rome—the beloved of God, called saints." Every Christian in Rome, not just a few, is the beloved of God, the called of God, a saint. The point is made even stronger when we realize that our calling is to sainthood, to be, literally, "holy ones." In other words, every Christian is sanctified, set apart by God's call as his.

"And we know that in all things God works for the good of those who love him, who have been called according to his purpose" (Rom. 8:28). Once again, we note the unlimited application of God's call. The promise of this verse is not for some small number of elite Christians; rather it applies to all Christians who are, by definition, called according to his purpose.

"God, who has called you into fellowship with his Son Jesus Christ our Lord, is faithful" (1 Cor. 1:9). All of us, not some of us, were called.

"I, therefore, the prisoner of the Lord, beseech you to walk worthy of the calling with which you were called" (Eph. 4:1 NKJV). Both as a noun and as a verb, *call* is applied to all believers.

The word for *call* in the New Testament is *kaleo*. It can be translated as *calling, vocation,* or *invitation.* After examining every verse that uses the word, I came to this working definition: the call of God is an authoritative, divine invitation with a purpose.

In other words, there is an invitation from God that carries power and authority; it is not like some wedding invitation to which we may decide how we RSVP. God is calling. God is speaking. The invitation is powerful. It is authoritative. It demands an answer. It even contains the power with which to answer. Indeed, my sense from Scripture is that it is much harder to resist God's call than to answer it.

The other aspect of the call is that God calls us to something or for something. He invites us for a reason. In Scripture, God calls us to be his people and possession, to be holy, to be saints, to experience fellowship with Christ, to serve him only, and to expand his kingdom on this earth.

Do you know God's call on your life? Have you accepted his authoritative invitation? Can you express your purpose under God? If God made Eric Liddell to be fast so that he could honor God through running, what has he made you for?

Business Is a High Calling from God

For me, the answer to each of the preceding questions is business. God called me to business, just as he's called missionaries, teachers, nurses, and physicians to their respective professions. In my life I have known the sense of God's call in two distinct areas. I was called to be a pastor for a period and later called into business.

As Dallas Willard put it:

It is as great and as difficult a *spiritual* calling to run the factories and the mines, the banks and the department stores, the schools and government agencies for the Kingdom of God as it is to pastor a church or serve as an evangelist.[2]

How do we know that business is a calling from God? I would answer with a question. Why wouldn't it be? If we believe that God's call is for all believers and affects all aspects of life, why would business be the one vocation that we refuse to acknowledge as anointed by God?

Now let me take this a step further and say that business not only is a calling from God, as legitimate as any other, but also like all of God's callings, is both high and holy. Not only are there no distinctions in Scripture between the called and the uncalled (at least not among Christians), but there are also no distinctions between those whose calling is high and those whose calling is low or not so high.

Once again, the sacred-secular dichotomy rears its ugly head. Scripture is clear that all are called. Nevertheless, many still maintain some kind of distinctions within the body of Christ by referring to degrees or levels of calling. Put another way, some are called and others are *really* called.

I recall my days in Bible-training school during the mid-1970s. Even though no one ever said these words or anything like them, the students caught the belief that the highest calling they could receive was to go overseas as a missionary. If God didn't call them to missions, the next highest calling was to the pastorate, then to teach in a Christian school, and so on down the list until you got to the bottom and took a secular job. What was even more damaging was the conviction that the further you got down the list, the lower the level of your calling, the less useful to God you were—and the implication was that it was your fault! There is so much wrong with this kind of thinking. Suffice it to say that the idea of degrees of calling based on one's value to God is a bondage hard to shake and leaves the body of Christ fragmented and frustrated. Further, it creates a breeding ground for depression, division, and pride.

---

2. Willard, *The Spirit of the Disciplines*, 214 (italics in original).

However, if we accept that the very highest thing we can do with our lives is to do that for which God made us, that is, to follow his call, we are immediately free from this false religious thinking, this sacred-secular split, this floating guilt that if we loved God more we'd enjoy a higher call. Instead, we are free to pour our whole hearts into God's plan for our lives and to embrace our calling—whatever it is—with every fiber of our being.

How do I know this? I know this because there is no better path for anyone than God's path, no greater plan than God's plan. In Romans 12, Paul tells us that in response to God's grace in our lives, we are to offer our bodies and our lives to him without reservation. "Living sacrifices" is what he calls this (Rom. 12:1). Once we offer ourselves to God, we begin to be changed and to learn his will for our lives; Paul refers to this will, or calling, as "perfect" (Rom. 12:2). So if God has called you to business and you are sure of that call, that is the highest possible calling there could be. Preaching could not be higher for you. Missions could not be higher for you. Why? Because for you they would not be perfect. Only God's will is perfect.

Conclusion

The very first aspect of building and leading a kingdom business is knowing that you are called to it. A kingdom business is vocational. It is based on a confidence that business is a good thing and that God has called you to this enterprise. Everything else flows from this reality.

The good news is that believers are called to it. All Christians have a calling, a high and holy calling. Business is mine. Is it yours? If so, pursue it with all your heart for the glory of God and always remember that God made you for a purpose that includes business, and when you do business, you honor him.

A KINGDOM BUSINESS IS
INTENTIONAL

3

BEYOND PROFIT: DEFINING
YOUR KINGDOM PURPOSE

As a physician, Lee used his profession as an outreach for Christ. He worked at his practice, he worked in the inner city, and he worked behind the Iron Curtain. Then, in a series of circumstances that only God could orchestrate, Lee ended up at an important dinner in Washington, D.C. His table partner was the Minister of Health for one of the newly independent Soviet republics. By the end of dinner, Lee had been invited to the man's country to provide medical technology and training and to help reform the nation's fledgling healthcare system. Since that fateful meeting, Lee has been used of God to found an agency that has sent hundreds of medical teams to Central Asia—all sharing the love of Christ.

Lee is a great example of a devoted follower of Christ who has learned to link his profession to an eternal purpose. He has become intentional in his work and has connected his business to something greater than profit. For kingdom professionals, discovering a sense of mission for our lives and work that flows from understanding God's mission is essential.

For decades companies have been spending enormous amounts of money and time developing "mission statements" or "purpose statements." These attempts to define why the business exists turn out results that vary from short, pithy slogans (e.g., "pizza in thirty minutes or it's free—Domino's") to long and meaningless statements (usually claiming some sort of world-class status in their industry and generating benefit to employees, community, and shareholders). In my opinion, few are actually of any value—except to the consulting firm that was paid to generate them. Company leaders pay little attention to mission statements when making decisions, and employees treat them as a joke, a sort of plaque du jour.

Nevertheless, every business does have a purpose and should identify what it is. Articulating it in a way that is accurate, clear, and motivating is vital to the success and sustainability of any organization.[1]

You may recall the scene from *Alice in Wonderland* in which Alice comes to a fork in the road. Confused as to which way to turn, she is surprised by the appearance of the Cheshire Cat. He asks, "What is your problem?" Alice replies, "I don't know which road to take." The Cat asks in return, "Where are you going?" "I don't know," says Alice. The Cat then says, "Then it really doesn't matter which road you take!" In the same way, a clear statement of purpose is necessary in helping a company make decisions, for example: Does this opportunity help us achieve our mission? Will it take us where we want to go?

What is the purpose of your business? Management guru Peter Drucker has stated unequivocally that the purpose of business is to make money. Consultant Brian Tracy says that business exists to attract and retain customers. Who is right? In a sense, they are both right and both incomplete. Businesses do exist to make money, and of course there is no way to make money without attracting and retaining customers. But is that all there is?

According to Scripture, there is a purpose that is beyond profit and beyond customers. There is a kingdom purpose—a way in which

---

1. Specifically, I would advocate involving in the actual writing of the mission statement the people being asked to embrace the mission; in this way companies can be sure that what is generated will be authentic and meaningful.

the business specifically and intentionally connects to the growth of God's kingdom in the world and thus brings glory to him. The goal of this chapter is to explore what God says about purpose and to begin the process of discovering, articulating, and implementing the specific kingdom purpose for which he led you to your business.

God Is a Teleological God

Teleology is the study of purposes and end results. Thus, when we say that God is a teleological God, we are recognizing that he is a God of purpose and plans, that he has an end in mind for the things he does and creates. This is a comforting truth because it answers the great questions of life: Do I have a purpose? Is there a reason I am here? Is there a plan for this life? The answer from Scripture is a resounding yes!

Consider the following verses:

Then God said, "Let us make man in our image, in our likeness, and let them rule over the fish of the sea and the birds of the air, over the livestock, over all the earth, and over all the creatures that move along the ground." (Gen. 1:26)

"For I know the plans I have for you," declares the LORD, "plans to prosper you and not to harm you, plans to give you hope and a future." (Jer. 29:11)

And we know that in all things God works for the good of those who love him, who have been called according to his purpose. For those God foreknew he also predestined to be conformed to the likeness of his Son, that he might be the firstborn among many brothers. (Rom. 8:28–29)

In him we were also chosen, having been predestined according to the plan of him who works out everything in conformity with the purpose of his will. (Eph. 1:11)

Each of these verses speaks clearly about plans and purposes. God made humanity for a purpose that includes ruling over creation. God has plans for each of us to bring us to an expected future. God's purpose for us is to be made like Christ through the process of sanctification. And God is working in all things to bring about his purpose, his plans.

God is a purposeful God. He has plans. He is teleological. He has purposes *for us*. There is an end result *for us*. God is not random, and neither are we. Therefore, life has meaning: to discover and do the purpose of God.

God Established Business for a Purpose

If God is a purposeful, teleological God, the things he creates are somehow related to his plan. If they are related to his plan, these things have purposes of their own that are bestowed by him. Business is one of these things. If we acknowledge that God created business (just as he created the family, the church, and governments), there is a purpose (or purposes) for it.

At the grandest level, we can safely say that business exists to contribute to God's ultimate purpose—to bring him glory. It also exists to contribute to the major initiatives that support this overall purpose: the ruling and stewardship of creation, the salvation of individuals, the sanctification of believers, and the transformation of society. What an enriching view of business! We can recognize and take great encouragement in the reality that business does not exist for itself nor is it an end in itself. Rather, business is a part of God's orchestration and constant movement toward a glorious and eternal end, a result that will see him honored and worshiped by every nation.

God also ordained other purposes for business, as outlined in chapter 1. These purposes include provision for our families, for the poor, for the church, and for relationships.

As in all things, God has a purpose for business. Business is not something people dreamed up to gain wealth or to control others (though certainly after the Fall that is what it has often become). Instead, it is a divine institution with a divine purpose.

God Established Your Business for a Purpose

Psalm 139 states the following regarding God's creation of and interest in each of us:

> For you created my inmost being;
>   you knit me together in my mother's womb.
> I praise you because I am fearfully and wonderfully made;
>   your works are wonderful,
>   I know that full well.
> My frame was not hidden from you
>   when I was made in the secret place.
> When I was woven together in the depths of the earth,
>   your eyes saw my unformed body.
> All the days ordained for me
>   were written in your book
>   before one of them came to be. (vv. 13–16)

From before time God knew us. In our conception his mighty, creative action was applied to us. He made us wonderfully, exactly as he purposed. Does it not follow that with such an interest in our births he would have an equal interest in our lives?

The interest of God in our lives is a theme of the entire Bible. We are placed by birth in a specific location and a time sovereignly chosen by him (see Acts 17:26). The very hairs on our heads are numbered by God himself, as are the days we shall live on the earth (see Matt. 10:30, Ps. 139:16). The day of our death is appointed, as are also the details of every moment we live. God takes a supreme interest in us.

The Bible is even more specific. Not only is God interested in our lives, but he has a plan for us as well. He has a purpose for our lives, our families, and our businesses. Yes, he has a plan, not merely for business but for each of our businesses, as we can see in Ephesians 2:10: "For we are God's workmanship, created in Christ Jesus to do good works, which God prepared in advance for us to do." In a very real sense, we can see that God has set out a plan for each of our lives and for each of our businesses; it is a part of his overall plan and is orchestrated together with all things to bring about his ultimate purpose. No wonder that Paul prays for the Philippian believers that they would be filled with the knowledge of God's will (see Phil. 1:9–11).

Do you know what that will is? If God's purposes give meaning to life, the obvious and most pressing quest of your life should be to discover his purpose for you. Why did he make you? Why did he call you into this life, into this business? The answers to those questions go far beyond merely giving a sense of meaning and peace to your existence, they give strategic importance to your existence because you can be assured that your life and everything in it has a vital part to play in God's eternal plan, in the unfolding of his kingdom on earth.

So I will ask again, do you know what God's kingdom purpose is for your business? What lies beyond profit for your business?

We Are to Discover Our Kingdom Purpose

Some will say that discovering and doing the will of God is the key to personal happiness and fulfillment. This is true in a sense, of course. However, how would this emphasis on personal meaning fit into the lives of men like Stephen, Elijah, and Jeremiah—men who suffered much while knowing and doing God's will? Consider those who followed God's purpose for their lives and yet suffered greatly in that pursuit (see Heb. 11). Others will say that knowing the kingdom purpose of your business legitimizes it. To them I would say that business needs no legitimization. As part of God's calling and creation, business is already legitimate.

Ultimately, the true reason for seeking to discover and implement God's kingdom purpose for your business is that doing so is the mark of a true disciple. Jesus said that if anyone would be his disciple the requirement is "deny himself and take up his cross daily and follow" him (Luke 9:23). Simply put, that means that a true follower must displace his or her own plans and purposes, accept the full will of God, whatever the implications, and wholeheartedly pursue that will. It means that disciples who are business owners are to set aside their own purposes and submit fully to God's purposes for their enterprises. It is this action, more than any other, that distinguishes a kingdom company from a company run by Christians. Kingdom business is intentional.

So how does one discover God's kingdom purpose for a business? To many Christians the idea of discovering and doing the will of God is a matter of great mystery and even greater uncertainty. Christian business leaders are not exempt from this dilemma. What is encouraging to understand is that God is even more committed to your knowing his will and doing it than you are! It should come as no surprise, then, that the Scriptures are filled with instruction on how this discovery takes place. Following are a few of the principles found in the Bible.

God's purposes are primarily revealed in the written Word. I have known many Christians who have spent countless months or years seeking to discover some mysterious plan from God for their lives. Fortunately, virtually everything we need to know is already laid out for us in God's Word. Consider the following verses:

> The secret things belong to the LORD our God, but the things revealed belong to us and to our children forever, that we may follow all the words of this law. (Deut. 29:29)

> He has showed you, O man, what is good.
> And what does the LORD require of you?
> To act justly and to love mercy
> and to walk humbly with your God. (Mic. 6:8)

> All Scripture is God-breathed and is useful for teaching, rebuking, correcting and training in righteousness, so that the man of God may be thoroughly equipped for every good work. (2 Tim. 3:16–17)

> His divine power has given us everything we need for life and godliness through our knowledge of him who called us by his own glory and goodness. Through these he has given us his

very great and precious promises, so that through them you may participate in the divine nature and escape the corruption in the world caused by evil desires. (2 Pet. 1:3–4)

Examining these verses brings us to a solid reality: the will of God is found in the Word of God. Therefore, any search for a kingdom purpose should be focused there.

The knowledge of the will of God is given to those willing and ready to do it. It is not as if God allows us to "sample" his will in advance and then decide whether we will accept it or not. Why would God submit himself to our caprice as if he were some kind of cosmic salesman? On the contrary, there is a very clear sequence taught in the Word: submission, then revelation; surrender, then clarity. It is not the other way around. Consider carefully the words of Paul in addressing the Romans: "Therefore, I urge you, brothers, in view of God's mercy, to *offer your bodies as living sacrifices,* holy and pleasing to God—this is your spiritual act of worship. Do not conform any longer to the pattern of this world, but be transformed by the renewing of your mind. *Then you will be able to test and approve what God's will is*—his good, pleasing and perfect will" (Rom. 12:1–2, emphasis added).

The order is clear. In light of all that God has done for us in Christ (outlined in the first eleven chapters of Romans), we are called to surrender ourselves without reservation to him. He is the Lord and we are the disciples, the followers. We embrace his authority and offer our bodies in a "no strings attached" transaction. We are his! Then, as a part of the process that flows from that commitment, we are changed and we begin to learn, to know, to understand by experience what God's will is.

The application is clear. If we would know God's purpose for our lives and for our businesses, we must turn our lives and our businesses over to him. Only then will he begin to work to let us in on the plan that he has for us.

Understanding the purposes of God is a matter of illumination by his Spirit. This third foundational principle is essential to our understanding God's will. Even though God's will is primarily contained within the Word, without the illuminating ministry of the Holy Spirit in our lives, the Word is just as incomprehensible to us as Jesus' parables were to the multitudes. That is why, on two different occasions, Paul is found praying that God's Spirit would work in the hearts and minds of believers to give them spiritual understanding of God and his truth.

Writing to the church in Ephesus, Paul records this prayer: "I keep asking that the God of our Lord Jesus Christ, the glorious Father, may give you the Spirit of wisdom and revelation, so that you may know him better. I pray also that the eyes of your heart may be enlightened in order that you may know the hope to which he has called you" (Eph. 1:17–18). In Colossians Paul writes, "We have not stopped praying for you and asking God to fill you with the knowledge of his will through all spiritual wisdom and understanding" (Col. 1:9). Clearly, it is not enough to search the Word (much less try to figure it out on our own). It is not enough to want to know God's will and be submitted to doing it. We must also have the illumination of the Holy Spirit if we are to actually understand.

So we see a pattern. The purposes of God are revealed in the Word to those who are fully surrendered to him and who are enabled by the Holy Spirit to understand what they read.

How, then, does one discover God's kingdom purpose for a business? What specific steps can one take? There are several keys, each of which plays a part.

1. *Pray.* It is in prayer that we arrive at the place of submission and willingness to learn what God has in store for us. Jesus taught us to pray "Thy kingdom come. Thy will be done in earth, as *it is* in heaven" (Matt. 6:10, KJV). It is in constant prayer that we come to understand the heart and purpose of God.

2. *Read and meditate on Scripture.* Instead of the normal approach to devotions in which we read to get a "word from the Lord" or have some verse stand out to us, go to the Word with a quest: "Show me your will, O Lord, for

my business." Learn to live a life saturated with the truth of God's Word. As we are filled with the truths of the Word, our understanding of his purposes will be formed.

3. *Meet with others who know their kingdom purpose.* Solomon said, "As iron sharpens iron, so one man sharpens another" (Prov. 27:17). The point is that in fellowship and discussion with others who are searching after the kingdom impact of their businesses, you are more likely to find yours.

4. *Expose yourself to what God is doing in the world.* God is at work in the world every day. Seek out what he is doing and where he is doing it. Go on short-term mission trips, visit established kingdom companies at home or overseas, build a Habitat for Humanity house, serve in a soup kitchen, or contact business leaders who have seen God at work in their firms. It is where God is at work that you are most likely to discover where he wants you to work. Don't be afraid of mistakes or even of failures. Ultimately, there are no mistakes in God's kingdom—only opportunities to better learn his ways.

5. *Keep a journal.* This is a great exercise in general and incredibly helpful in tracing the things God is teaching you and the ways in which he is communicating his will to you.

6. *Write a kingdom impact statement.* Try to put into words what you believe God has shown you to date. It is likely that it will change over time, but the discipline of putting your thoughts on paper will help you crystallize what God is saying to you.

7. *Repeat steps 1–6.* I'm not trying to be cute. As you seek God's purpose for your business, you will find that the picture becomes clearer over time, and the vision will mature as you mature. This is a process that will continue for the rest of your life.

Conclusion

Live a life realizing the plan God has for you. To be ignorant of the fact that the sovereign, all-wise Lord of the universe has a specific purpose for you to fulfill is the epitome of emptiness. God is purposeful in all he does—in creation, in ruling the universe, and in calling you to business. Seek with all your heart to know and fulfill his kingdom purpose for you.

4

KINGDOM PURPOSE LIVED OUT

When I first started my company, I thought its purpose was to provide me with the flexibility and finances to pursue business development work in Central Asia. Little did I know that God's real purpose was to begin the process of multiplying kingdom companies around the world. From beginnings in one country we have expanded to over twenty, and our graduates' companies number in the hundreds.

One of my greatest frustrations is thinking small. I do it. Most of us do it. It limits us in life and it certainly limits us in living for Christ. This is surprisingly true of business owners when it comes to exploring God's purpose for their companies. You would think that men and women accustomed to entrepreneurial and expansive thoughts would be entrepreneurial and expansive in identifying their kingdom purpose. Unfortunately, what I often hear as "kingdom impact" is no more innovative or out of the box than increased giving or establishing a Bible study for employees.

I believe there is more to God's plan for each of our businesses than the ordinary. By taking a larger look, we can be captured by a larger kingdom purpose. As the great missionary William Carey said,

"Expect great things from God; attempt great things for God." This chapter is about doing just that.

Connecting Our Purpose to God's Purpose

As we seek to know God's plan for our businesses, we will not discover some secret verse written just for us, nor will we find some strange code that unlocks the mysteries of Scripture. We will likely not have a dramatic vision of our company's future. What will happen is that as we delve into the Word, seek the guidance of the Holy Spirit, and thoughtfully pursue an understanding of God's plan for us, we will begin to see the purposes of God that have always been there—unchangeable from the beginning of time. And as we more deeply understand and identify with God's great plan for the world and humanity, the manner in which we connect to that plan will become increasingly apparent. This connection is, in essence, our kingdom purpose.

The Scriptures are very clear and repetitive when it comes to God's purpose for humanity and for creation. There are not many purposes but one overarching purpose that unites everything. What is it? From before the foundation of the earth God has planned to fill the earth with people who know and honor him. It is in this way that all of his attributes, such as wisdom, kindness, grace, and majesty, are demonstrated and appreciated. In other words, it is all for his glory, and he did this because it pleased him. When God created Adam and Eve, he gave the following charge: "Be fruitful and increase in number; fill the earth and subdue it" (Gen. 1:28). In simple terms, God told them to have children and begin the process of populating the earth with people just like them—people made in God's image, people who know and honor God, and people who experience fellowship with their Creator. In this way, they and all their descendants would be blessed, and he would be glorified. It couldn't be simpler. God created the earth with the purpose of having it filled with his worshipers. Unfortunately, humanity rebelled against God's rule, became a fallen race, and systematically filled the earth with the very opposite of what God intended, with those who do not know him or honor him. This is what the apostle Paul describes when he says that although humanity "knew [about] God, they neither glorified him as God nor gave thanks to him…. [T]hey…exchanged the glory of the immortal God for images made to look like mortal man and birds and animals and reptiles…. They exchanged the truth of God for a lie, and worshiped and served created things rather than the Creator" (Rom. 1:21–25).

Nevertheless, while humanity has changed, God's purpose for humanity has not. No matter how far the world may be from what God desires, his plan remains the same as in the beginning. Now, however, our sin stands in the way. Sin must be paid for—the biblical term is *atoned for*. And that, of course, is where the gospel comes in. God the Creator removed the sin that separates us from him through the substitutionary death, burial, and resurrection of his Son, the Lord Jesus Christ. In and through Christ, men and women are called back to God, brought into relationship with him, blessed by him, and enabled to worship him. In Christ, God's unchangeable purpose for us is realized. And this purpose still remains as Christ, through us, seeks out the lost of this world to be his own. Indeed, shortly after his resurrection, Jesus gave this instruction to his followers: "Therefore go and make disciples of all nations, baptizing them in the name of the Father and of the Son and of the Holy Spirit, and teaching them to obey everything I have commanded you" (Matt. 28:19–20). Note that this passage, commonly called the Great Commission, is essentially the same thing that God told Adam and Eve to do—populate the earth with God's worshipers. It is not new. It is not revolutionary. It is consistent. Indeed, the Scriptures, rightly read, are totally consistent on this point. This is God's purpose—his kingdom purpose.

And lest you have any question about the changeability of God's purposes, take a look at Revelation 7:9. This is how it ends. John records, "After this I looked and there before me was a great multitude that no one could count, from every nation, tribe, people and language, standing before the throne and in front of the Lamb."

So we see God's purpose: to fill up the earth with people who know and love him and, in this way, to glorify himself while blessing his creation. This is his plan and his desired end result. Our purpose, our kingdom purpose, should mirror this and be connected to it in some way.

Ever-Expanding Circles of Influence

For many of us, the idea of connecting our business to God's kingdom purpose is, at least, daunting and perhaps overwhelming and discouraging. Jesus knows this just as he knew it when he spoke to his disciples. That is why, I believe, he further clarified the mission in Acts 1. Here, as before, the resurrected Christ was speaking his heart for the world to a handful of poorly qualified individuals. He told them to wait in Jerusalem until they received power from God through the Holy Spirit (see Acts 1:4–5). However, when the power came, they were to launch out in a series of ever-expanding circles of influence. For them, this meant geography. "But you will receive power when the Holy Spirit comes on you; and you will be my witnesses in Jerusalem, and in all Judea and Samaria, and to the ends of the earth" (Acts 1:8). There was no mystery here for the disciples. They were to begin "repopulating the earth" with worshipers where they were and from there to gradually move out in ever-expanding circles of influence.

The same is true for us—not necessarily geographically but practically. We do not live in Jerusalem, so we cannot use this as a specific guide, nor can we, as some have attempted, simply reposition Jerusalem on our map and work out from there. Rather, we should grasp the principle of starting where we are and moving farther and deeper into connection with God's cosmic purposes. Perhaps it does mean geography for us. Perhaps it means ever-widening circles of relationships. Perhaps it speaks to us of beginning with what is readily apparent and gradually moving to a global impact over time. I don't believe there is any right or wrong here but rather a course of thought. In other words, I believe that the idea of kingdom impact begins with the question, "What can I do for Christ's kingdom with what is immediately at hand?" and moves over time and maturity to the larger question, "What can I do for Christ's kingdom in the world?" and ultimately to "What can I do for Christ's kingdom among those who are unreached?" The point is this: our purpose can be said to be a kingdom purpose only if it is connected to God's kingdom purpose. It is required of us that we search out the connection between our business and what God is doing in the world (near to us and far away) and then, in reliance on the Holy Spirit's power, step out to fulfill that unique purpose for which God has called us. All over the world, business owners are connecting their companies to God's kingdom purpose. Their kingdom purposes may continue to evolve, but they have begun to influence people for God, whether in a single community or across an industry. Let me give a couple of examples.

Joseph started a motorcycle repair shop in a predominantly Muslim village in Asia. He understood God's heart to show mercy to the lost, and as he looked at this particular village, he realized that it had no gospel witness at all. Its people were entirely unreached. His business gave him a reason to be there that did not arouse suspicions that he was some kind of missionary and actually enabled him to establish relationships with Muslims. This became his kingdom purpose—to live and work among Muslims and, through words and the way he conducted business, to share Christ's love with them. The latest report I received on Joseph was that a local imam (a Muslim holy man) was telling people that Joseph was the only person he could recommend for motorcycle repairs because he was an honest, Christian man.

Another example is Mira, a young woman from Central Asia. After coming to Christ, Mira wanted a way to share the gospel with other young women. She launched a handicraft manufacturing business that gathers young women into her home. Her kingdom purpose is to effectively communicate the gospel through an informal work environment. As they work together, Mira is able to talk with her employees about the gospel and the difference that Jesus has made in her life.

One U.S. engineering firm I know of established a biblically based supervisory training program, tactfully but boldly explaining that its philosophy of business was built on God's Word. The firm's kingdom purpose is to create a nurturing environment where God's care for people is demonstrated.

Or what about an Atlanta-based construction company that offers a weekly Bible study to its employees, with no pressure to attend? The owner explained to me that he sees his employees as a divine responsibility; offering an optional time to study the Word fits in with that responsibility.

On a global level, there is Pura Vida Coffee Company. Pura Vida is a coffee-importing company set up by Christians who were led to address the social injustices of business in Central America. By eliminating the middleman, Pura Vita is able to pay a better price to poor coffee growers, establish credibility for its gospel witness, and sell its product profitably in the United States.

Spheres of Life

One way to slice this question of kingdom purpose is to examine it in light of the spheres of life or the various parts of life we touch. What are our various roles and relationships? Are we husband, father, wife, mother, son, daughter, employer, executive, vendor, customer, church member, citizen? The ensuing question would then be, How might God use us and our business in these various roles and relationships? A simple way to think this through is to ask the following question of each role and relationship you fill through business, substituting each role and relationship in turn for the word *employees*:

What might God's purpose be in the three-way connection between my business, my employees, and his eternal purpose of filling up the world with worshipers and transforming society into the kingdom of Christ? The answer might be to establish a corporate chaplaincy program, as one of my clients is doing. The idea is to provide a pastoral ministry to her employees who might not go to church anywhere. They would be cared for, prayed for, and loved right on the job.

What could his purpose be in the three-way connection between my international consulting firm, my clients who live in communist countries, and God's plan? The answer might be to establish a ministry of prayer for targeted people, by name, in these countries and to systematically seek out ways to introduce them to the gospel. Meeting and getting to know the lost through my business creates opportunities for intercession and witness.

In what way could God use my business relationships as a customer to my suppliers to impact them for his kingdom? The answer might be to use prompt payment policies to establish credibility for future conversations about Christianity.

As we work through this process, we can begin to get a sense of what God's purpose might be in each of the areas and also seek for a composite or blended purpose that unites them all. For example, the apostle Paul expressed his own overarching kingdom purpose this way: "We proclaim him [Christ], admonishing and teaching everyone with all wisdom, so that we may present everyone perfect in Christ. To this end I labor, struggling with all his energy, which so powerfully works in me" (Col. 1:28–29).

The Institutions of Society

Another way to examine the question of kingdom purpose is to consider its direct and indirect impact upon various societal institutions. If God's intention is to transform society, it follows, then, that he will most likely do this through impacting and transforming the pillars of society.

There are as many as seven institutions that God considers pillars of society: the family, the church, the government, enterprise (business), the arts, the media, and academia. Each pillar or institution contributes to the character and stability (or instability) of a society. The health of and reverence for family and marriage are critical to the character of a society, as we witness daily in our own declining culture. The church, as salt and light (Matt. 5:13–16), is meant to support, influence, and impact society by speaking God's truth and exhibiting God's character to believers and unbelievers alike. Government is instituted by God to influence and control the dispensation of justice in human interactions. Enterprise is God's appointed means for wealth creation and provides the economic engine for the other pillars. The arts express humanity's creative and celebratory nature as received from our Creator God, both influencing and reflecting society at large. The media encompass the organs of communication—electronic and print—a clear influence on any society. Academia, the education of the next generation, is the final pillar and exerts a profound influence on a society's values and behaviors. Each of these pillars is connected to the others. For me, from a business perspective, the question, then, is how can business, or more specifically, my business, impact the institutions God has created in a way that ultimately impacts society for Christ.

As with the spheres of life, we can use a simple question-based formula to seek out God's kingdom purpose for our businesses:

In what ways might my business life and position interact with or influence the pillar of government? I know of one brother who uses his international business as a way of reaching into the governments of Muslim countries. The friendships that he forms with these leaders are both conduits for the gospel and the means of influencing national policy in directions of righteousness and tolerance of Christianity.

In what ways can my company impact academia and the education of young people for Christ? Michelle, a close business associate of mine, has offered an annual scholarship to students at a Christian graduate school. The condition for winning the award is writing a white paper on business as mission. In this way, Michelle is exposing future leaders to the concept of kingdom business as well as increasing the amount of research and writing available on the subject.

Prayerfully considering these questions will help us discover the kingdom purpose for which God created our businesses.

The Geography of the World

The third perspective from which we might deduce our kingdom purpose is geography or, more accurately, geopolitics. Let's look once again at the instruction of Jesus to his disciples in Acts 1:8: "And you will be my witnesses in Jerusalem, and in all Judea and Samaria, and to the ends of the earth." The disciples were to begin where they were and gradually work their way outward until Christ was known all over the earth, to the "uttermost part" (KJV). This was a brilliant strategy. Begin with what is at hand and what is near you. Then, with intentionality, move outward to the next closest geographical setting and so on until all peoples in all places have heard the gospel and disciples have been made from all peoples (see Matt. 28:19–20).

A business that seeks to be a kingdom business may once again use the question method to think through geographical impact:

How might my business be used by God to fulfill his ultimate purpose in my hometown? The answer might be to fund a local ministry to the homeless, to employ and train welfare recipients, or to provide tutors at a local elementary school.

How could my construction firm be part of what God is doing in my state? Perhaps you could align your company with a faith-based ministry like Habitat for Humanity that builds affordable housing for the poor. Clearly there are local impact opportunities very near to home. There are also opportunities a bit farther out, and even in other similar-culture countries. Have you thought through them? Could this be your kingdom purpose?

The Hard-to-Reach Places

The final grid to examine is a subset, but a strategically vital subset, of the overall geographical or geopolitical perspective. I refer to those countries where traditional missionary activity is neither possible nor particularly effective.

Consider the following reality. To date, there are still over two thousand unreached people groups in the world, that is, entire cultures where there is no viable Christian witness, no sustainable kingdom presence. Most of these are found in countries that are at best resistant and at worst hostile to direct, overt missionary activity. Many are Muslim-controlled lands. Some are Hindu or Buddhist. Some remain in the atheistic Communist camp. Here is the "uttermost part" of our day, and here the traditional missionary messenger of the kingdom cannot enter. Missiologists call these *closed* or *restricted-access* countries.

Yet each of these countries is open to the involvement of real businesses led by real businesspeople. Visas and government cooperation are freely flowing to those who, through legitimate and actual business operations, bring wealth, employment, and development to their people. This provides a unique and critical opportunity for the kingdom professional. We can ask ourselves, "Could it be that there is some way to use my business to enter a closed country, to build relationships with the people, and through those relationships have direct and indirect impact on the society for Christ?" The answer is a resounding yes!

Once again, we use the question method:

How can God use my real business to impact a restricted country for his glory? One U.S. company has opened a factory in a closed country that manufactures a unique product used in construction projects around the world. This business provides jobs for locals at fair pay, a decent work environment, and regular interaction with Christian managers who have committed to live for Christ in this particular country.

My own belief is that we are on the edge of a huge movement of God to mobilize true professionals to engage in these hard-to-reach places. Many cannot go. Many will not go. But the kingdom professional can and will as God leads—and many already have gone. Here are a few examples of ways that kingdom business is being used around the world.

Some have been led into using business training—sharing their own knowledge and experience of business through seminars—to reach out to those who live in the difficult places. Using teams of volunteer business leaders, these groups conduct seminars in places such as Ukraine as a means of outreach. This is an indirect engagement, but it is a way that kingdom professionals can use their businesses to impact the world for Christ.

Others have taken the concept of business training, which is essentially a way for business leaders to plug into missions, a step further and established business-development ministries. These combine training, coaching, and funding provided through Christian volunteers to actually help locals start their own businesses. While most of these works, like the one in which I am involved, focus on believers, there are some that use enterprise development as a means of outreach directly to the lost. Like seminar training, for many this type of approach is an indirect involvement of their companies, since they are essentially leaving their businesses behind and taking their business experience to the mission field through a third-party agency. For others, however, it can be a direct engagement. In that case, the owner of the company uses the company, personnel, and financial resources to set up microenterprise operations in another country. The latter is the way my company does this; my for-profit consulting firm focuses profits overseas and provides flexible employment solutions for our associates so that they can involve themselves in microenterprise among disenfranchised believers in unreached areas.

A much more direct engagement and a riskier enterprise is to actually open business operations in a foreign country. I know of several examples of U.S., European, Canadian, Korean, and Singaporean companies that have opened extension offices or factories in unreached areas. These are real, for-profit operations that provide employment, opportunity, training, and competitive benefits to national workers, that bring real value to the parent company through cost-effective manufacturing or service delivery, and that open doors of relationship through which both physical and spiritual blessings flow to locals. Many of these operate in restricted areas, so I won't name them, but they run the gamut of businesses, including manufacturing, call centers, credit unions, computer programming, engineering design, architecture, and product development.

A particular type of direct engagement through business that I believe has high potential is import-export. Most countries, open and restricted, have products that could be sold on the world market; however, many of these countries and their producers have little or no access to these markets. A Christian entrepreneur with distribution channels already in place will find a great opportunity in setting up collection, purchasing, and export businesses in restricted countries.

In addition to providing employment and much-needed income, this type of business offers direct involvement with people all over the country in which you work. I am privileged to serve on the board of directors of such a company that already has operations set up in several unreached areas and is constantly exploring new opportunities.

There is no end to what our creative God may come up with when kingdom business owners are submitted to his purpose and sincerely seek his purpose for their businesses. I have shared just a few ideas that I have seen. The point is that business is a great point of entry into these hard-to-reach places, and this may very well be the kingdom purpose for which God raised up your business.

Conclusion

Kingdom purpose is not necessarily discovered in the mysterious and mystical ways most often associated with knowing God's will. No one would approach any other business challenge that way. Instead, we take the known, in this case God's purpose, and the opportunity of impacting societies for Christ and the resources at our disposal and prayerfully think through the implications that present themselves to us. Then, with courage (see Josh. 1:9) and confidence in Christ's provision (see Matt. 28:20) we step out into the current of God's eternal plan. In this way, through discovering and implementing our kingdom purpose, we experience the intentionality of kingdom business.

3

A KINGDOM BUSINESS IS
RELATIONAL

5

THE PRIMACY OF RELATIONSHIPS

I could tell by the tone of voice in the message that something was different. Phil had come to know Christ! Through the course of our relationship, Phil had moved from client to friend. Now he had become a brother. Watching the change in him in the months that followed has been one of my greatest joys in business. Here was a man who would likely never have visited a church service, but he was now a follower of Jesus because of a business relationship.

As we read through Scripture, two things become patently clear: God is a God of relationship, and he has ordered his creation in such a way that above all things, relationships are of primary value and concern. He created humans for relationship with him (see Gen. 1:26; 3:8–9). He called Israel out of all the nations for relationship with him (see Deut. 6:4–5). Jesus called his followers to relationship with him (see Mark 3:13–14). The Holy Spirit today is still calling believers out of the world to have a relationship with God (see 1 Cor. 1:9). Clearly, God is a God of relationship and has called men and women into relationship with him.

This relational focus of God, however, is not solely focused on him; it is not only to a vertical relationship that God calls us but also to horizontal, interpersonal relationships. Even a cursory reading of the Gospel narratives will lead the student of Christ to recognize that the Master exemplified and taught the primacy of relationships between people in addition to the relationship between man and God. "Of all the commandments, which is the most important?" a religious leader asked Jesus. The Lord replied without hesitation, "The most important one…is…'Love the Lord your God with all your heart and with all your soul and with all your mind and with all your strength.' The second is this: 'Love your neighbor as yourself'" (Mark 12:28–31). In his farewell discourse the night before the crucifixion, the Lord told his disciples, "A new command I give you: Love one another. As I have loved you, so you must love one another. By this all men will know that you are my disciples, if you love one another" (John 13:34–35). Further reading of the epistles will reveal so many repeated uses of the phrase "one another" that we can easily conclude it is impossible to follow Christ on our own.

The truth is that the entire Bible speaks to relationship—with God, with fellow believers, and even with our enemies. We are told to love, to forgive, to serve, to assist, to support, to confront, to speak the truth to, to rebuke, to listen to…one another. Why is this so important? First, as we have seen, God is a God of relationship, so it follows that to be in relationship with others is one aspect of being like God. Second, and history bears this out, relationship is the primary means by which God spreads the magnificent influence of his reign upon the earth. This explains why we say that the third characteristic of a kingdom business is that it is relational—it is used of God within the various relationships it creates to further the interests of his kingdom on earth.

Relationships Are Fundamental to Life

Imagine a life without relationships: no friends, no family, no neighbors, and no fellow believers. Instead, we would live in total isolation from all other created beings without so much as an interaction. Frankly, this cannot be imagined, much less desired. Every human being, regardless of spiritual state, lives in the context of relationships. We are enmeshed in a web of interactions ranging from the ridiculous to the sublime, from the superficial to the intimate.

We did not choose most of these relationships. We were born into this already-existing web—our families, our neighborhoods, and our towns. From practically the moment of human creation it has always been so. In fact, after creating all things, including the first man, Adam, God said it was all good…except for one thing. Adam was alone. Kindly, God looked upon his creation and pronounced, "It is not good for the man to be alone" (Gen. 2:18). Consequently, to complete his act of creation, the Creator made woman to be with man and to be "a helper suitable for him" (Gen. 2:18–24) From that moment on, Adam was in relationship with another human by God's design, and "as it was in the beginning, is now and ever shall be, world without end, Amen!" In other words, by the sheer reality of our created state, we see that we were made for relationships.

When sin entered into the world (see Gen. 3), it damaged relationship more than anything. Humanity's relationship to God was broken, and the relationship to other humans was damaged. Adam and Eve, once innocent in their nakedness and openness to each other, now had to be clothed. Their children, Cain and Abel, ended up in such poor relationship with each other that one murdered the other. And so it has been ever since. Yet for all the damage within relationships, relationships do not go away. They may not function as intended, but they are still present. They are as fundamental to our humanity as our bodies or the physical world in which we live. To be outside of all relationships is to be less than human; to be human is to live in relationships.

Relationships Provide Kingdom Opportunities

History, Scripture, and even our own personal experience demonstrate that God's primary conduit for expressing himself in the world is through relationships. The influence of the gospel does not come through organizations but comes through human interaction, through a people-to-people process. We see this even with the first disciples:

> The next day John was there again with two of his disciples. When he saw Jesus passing by, he said, "Look, the Lamb of God!"

When the two disciples heard him say this, they followed Jesus. Turning around, Jesus saw them following and asked, "What do you want?"

They said, "Rabbi" (which means Teacher), "where are you staying?"

"Come," he replied, "and you will see."

So they went and saw where he was staying, and spent that day with him. It was about the tenth hour.

Andrew, Simon Peter's brother, was one of the two who heard what John had said and who had followed Jesus. The first thing Andrew did was to find his brother Simon and tell him, "We have found the Messiah" (that is, the Christ). And he brought him to Jesus.

Jesus looked at him and said, "You are Simon son of John. You will be called Cephas" (which, when translated, is Peter).

The next day Jesus decided to leave for Galilee. Finding Philip, he said to him, "Follow me."

Philip, like Andrew and Peter, was from the town of Bethsaida. Philip found Nathanael and told him, "We have found the one Moses wrote about." (John 1:35–45)

How was the influence of Christ's kingdom spread in this scenario? It was spread through a network of relationships. John spoke to his followers about Christ, and then they met the Savior and became his disciples. Jesus' first disciples then, through relationships, told their brothers and friends about the Messiah and they, in turn, became his followers. From this point on, the story of the expansion of the church follows the same pattern (although often through much larger expressions and larger crowds). Christ's kingdom and its power to transform societies are communicated through human interaction.

The Great Commission itself is built on this same principle. When Jesus spoke to his disciples in Matthew 28:18–20, he again called them to work through relationships. This is clearly implied when the phrase "Go therefore and make disciples" is more accurately translated "As you are in the process of going, disciple the

nations." Most of us have heard or read these words with an impera-
tive "go," as if it required crossing oceans, as if "going" was the point.
The word is actually a participle in Greek and carries the force of
process rather than command. The command is not "go"; "going" is
the process or means. The command is "disciple nations." In other
words, the main activity of discipling, leading others into a more obedient apprenticeship to Jesus, takes place in the context of walking
through life, that is, through the relationships of which life is made.

In my own life I can testify to the impact of relationship. To this
day, I thank God for a fellow student in college who befriended me
and, through that friendship, was instrumental in helping me come
to Christ. I had heard the gospel all my life, but it was through the
relationship that Richard built with me that God enabled me to actually understand and embrace salvation. I suspect that most Christians
can identify in some way with my experience.

Business Provides a Unique Matrix of Relationships

One of the most exciting aspects of business leadership as a Christian, as a discipler of men and women, and as a person committed to
societal transformation through the power of the gospel, is the amazing wealth of relationships (in business terms, "channels of distribution") that corporate interaction provides. Through the setting up of
business and its operation, God sovereignly and graciously provides
access to individuals whom we would otherwise never meet or spend
time with.

Early in my business career I taught a seminar in Canada on sta-
tistical process control. After the session, one of the managers,
Tommy, came up to me and asked to have dinner with me that night.
I agreed but asked him why he wanted to meet with me. Tommy
replied, "Because you know God and I don't." The dinner conversation was entirely about knowing Christ, and to this day I wonder
what part of that boring and technical seminar God used to awaken
Tommy's heart.

Each relationship in business is a fundamental part of our lives
and represents a special opportunity for kingdom impact. To illustrate

this point, think through the following matrix. Fill in the names of individuals within each box—you might be surprised how quickly you run out of room. Then ask yourself how many of these people you would have known, at whatever level of interaction, were it not for your business calling.

Business relationships

Relationship	Individuals
Shareholders/ Investors	
Employees	
Customers	
Vendors	
Competitors	
Colleagues	
Mentors/Mentees	
People in other lands	

As you can see, God has blessed you with a vast network of acquaintances with whom you share some level of community and with whom you have developed trust and intimacy. These people are in your world because of business, and each presents an open door for kingdom impact. To put it another way, these people and their connection to you form a stewardship from God. Care for it wisely.

Relational Impact Takes a Variety of Forms

Just as relationships exist along a continuum from mere awareness to profound intimacy, so can God's impact on them and through them on society be found in a sort of spectrum. Indeed, the work of discipling the nations is one vast continuum of divine activity.

Once again, examine the charter given to the church in Matthew 28:18–20. If interpreted in the fashion of the current tradition, along with correlated passages (see Luke 24:47–48, Mark 16:15, Acts 1:8), we end up with the idea that Christian ministry can be divided into two major components: evangelism and discipleship. The former refers to communicating the good news so as to win individuals to faith; the latter refers to those activities that mature these same individuals who have thus believed. This is indeed true and is a major part of the process. But it is not the whole story, nor is it the whole point—as if God desired only to save and disciple individuals.

Consider a more expansive and, I believe, more biblical interpretation. The whole of the charge given to his followers by Christ is to *disciple the nations*. This phrase covers everything that is in God's heart concerning the world and is tantamount to a call to see society transformed for the glory of God. Work with people, Jesus says, in all facets of life and in all manners of ways, to see that in them and through them the entire world is brought into submission to the Lordship of Christ. This is the great umbrella that covers all the activities in which the servant of Christ will be involved. It is discipling. It is discipling the nations.

With this expanded perspective—that the phrase "disciple the nations" refers to any and all activities and influence leading to the expansion of Christ's kingdom and total societal transformation—

we can think constructively about the various phases that may exist within it. The continuum runs from prekingdom activity to the final manifestation of the kingdom in all of its fullness. Every activity within the continuum, no matter how mundane, can be connected, directly or indirectly, to the kingdom itself. In this way we may speak in terms of the following:

- Prekingdom activities (establishing and developing relationships)
- Kingdom announcements (direct communication of the gospel, or evangelism)
- Kingdom orientation (immediate follow-up activities with new Christians, new initiates in the kingdom)
- Kingdom realization and application (activities and disciplines leading to maturity in matters of the kingdom and knowing Christ) (see Eph. 4:3–16)
- Kingdom manifestation (the activity of Christ to fully reveal his kingdom to the world in all of its glory)

This construction gives us a structured way to think about the relationships within our business networks. Not only are they relationships, but also each individual is at some point in the kingdom continuum. Thinking this way helps us to focus our relating, as well as our praying, in the context of relationships. For example, a customer might be an unbeliever who is, then, in the prekingdom stage of his life; our praying for him might be focused on opportunity to open conversations leading to the communication of the gospel. Or an employee might be a believer of many years with a reasonable level of maturity. She is in the kingdom-application stage. For this one we might pray in an entirely different way, or we might be led to invite her to a women's fellowship or simply be more transparent about what God is doing in our lives. Regardless of the stage, we can confidently do what we do and add a much greater degree of intentionality to our interactions with her.

There is no doubt Jesus "evaluated" his followers in much the same way. How else could he have said, "I have much more to say to you, more than you can now bear" (John 16:12)? Unlike Christ, we do not possess all wisdom and knowledge, so we cannot be entirely accurate. However, since our purpose is only to discern how to serve and love a person more intentionally and not to judge or condemn, our best guess is sufficient.

Take the time to think through the following adjusted matrix and identify the appropriate actions you should take.

Kingdom continuum matrix

Relationship	Individual	Kingdom Continuum Stage	Interaction/ Prayer
Shareholder	George S.	Kingdom orientation	Invite into 2:7[1] discipleship group
Employee	Mary W.	Prekingdom	Pray for opportunity to serve and earn the right to be heard
Customer	Joanne	Kingdom application	Invite to Perspectives class[2]

The blank matrix on the following page is meant for you to work through when you have more time. The ultimate point is not to fill out a form or even to use this for any length of time but to emphasize a way of thinking about life's relationships and the opportunities for kingdom impact.

---

1. The Navigators' 2:7 series, a discipleship program inspired by Colossians 2:7
2. "Perspectives on the World Christian Movement" is a dynamic course exploring what God is doing around the world and what we can do to further those purposes.

Kingdom continuum matrix

Relationship	Individual	Kingdom Continuum Stage	Interaction/ Prayer
Shareholders/ Investors			
Employees			
Customers			
Vendors			
Competitors			
Colleagues			
Mentors/ Mentees			
People in other lands			

Conclusion

With the understanding that God is a God of relationship, is it any surprise that he not only values relationships but also uses them strategically to realize his purposes in the world? As Christian business leaders, we have been blessed with an abundance of relationships—far beyond most people. How will we view them? As nuisances? As revenue streams or a chance to save money? Or as a blessing from God, an opportunity to infuse the life of another with kingdom impact?

I once asked an Indonesian Christian why the country had become so predominantly Muslim. Her answer illustrates the point of this whole chapter. She said that when the Western Christians came, primarily from Holland, they built missionary compounds and missionary churches and expected the Indonesian people to come to them. The Muslims, on the other hand, came as traders, farmers, merchants, and businesspeople and simply lived among the natives. Today, Indonesia is the world's most populous Muslim nation. I wonder how different it could have been?

6

CAN LOVE WORK IN BUSINESS?

"We've put you in our will," she said. I was amazed. Not many consultants are included in their clients' wills. Then she continued, "We've put you in it to run our company on behalf of our children until they are grown." I was more than amazed—I was stunned. It was one of the greatest honors anyone has ever given me. This couple, clients for several years, were expressing such a confidence in me that they were entrusting their company and their children's financial future into my hands.

My old business mentor used to say "Business is business and love is #%&#@%!!" In his mind there could be no mixing of the two. Business was played by a set of rules that had no room for love or anything like it. It was all about revenue and growth and profit and return on investment. Love simply didn't fit in.

This view might not pose a problem for an unbelieving business leader. Indeed, some can quickly justify their actions and attitudes with a flexible and situationally ethical system. They can put on their business hat and act one way, then get in the car, drive home, put on the family hat, and act in an entirely different way. To many there is no hypocrisy here at all. It's just business.

But what about the Christian? What about the disciple of Christ? Can we separate our lives like the unbeliever? Do we simply accept the same sacred-secular dichotomy, the same split thinking that says there are two worlds—church where Jesus rules and business where greed rules? Do we have an option to suspend our allegiance to Christ when we get to the office or to the factory? By definition as Christians, literally "Christ's ones," we are called to follow Christ, to imitate him, to do as he instructed. Otherwise we face the Lord's great question: "Why do you call me, 'Lord, Lord,' and do not do what I say?" (Luke 6:46). And the one thing he repeatedly told us to do was to love others.

A Quick Bible Survey

Just to get our bearings, let's take a quick survey of the teachings of Christ regarding love.

We are told to love our fellow Christians. We have no doubt about this command. Jesus clearly commands us to love one another, meaning other Christian brothers and sisters. In the Upper Room on the night before his crucifixion, Jesus gave these simple instructions to his followers: "A new command I give to you: Love one another. As I have loved you, so you must love one another. By this all men will know that you are my disciples, if you love one another" (John 13:34–35). Years later the apostle John, a man who was there that night, would take up this theme and devote an entire letter to the vital subject of Christians loving one another. In fact, he viewed this so strongly that he warned believers that only those who love their brothers and sisters are the ones who actually know and love God (1 John 4:7–8).

We are told to love those with whom we have little relationship. Earlier in his ministry, Jesus was confronted with a question regarding the Old Testament command to love your neighbor as yourself. "Who is my neighbor?" the questioner asked. In answer, Jesus told the famous parable of the Good Samaritan (Luke 10:25–37). The point of the story was clear—your neighbor was anyone to whom you had the chance to do good. It wasn't a matter of proximity or depth of relationship. A neighbor is essentially anyone with whom we have any level of relationship at all. Applied broadly, this means that we are to walk in love toward everyone and not just toward our friends or fellow believers.

We are told to love our enemies. Now Jesus is getting radical. It wasn't enough that Jesus commanded us to love our brothers and sisters or our families and friends. It wasn't enough to tell us to love those with whom we have little or no relationship. Jesus actually goes on to command us to love our enemies. It's worth looking at the entire passage to get the impact of what Jesus is saying:

> "But I tell you who hear me: Love your enemies, do good to those who hate you, bless those who curse you, pray for those who mistreat you. If someone strikes you on one cheek, turn to him the other also. If someone takes your cloak, do not stop him from taking your tunic. Give to everyone who asks you, and if anyone takes what belongs to you, do not demand it back. Do to others as you would have them do to you.
>
> "If you love those who love you, what credit is that to you? Even 'sinners' love those who love them. And if you do good to those who are good to you, what credit is that to you? Even 'sinners' do that. And if you lend to those from whom you expect repayment, what credit is that to you? Even 'sinners' lend to 'sinners' expecting to be repaid in full. But love your enemies, do good to them, and lend to them without expecting to get anything back. Then your reward will be great, and you will be sons of the Most High, because he is kind to the ungrateful and wicked. Be merciful, just as your Father is merciful." (Luke 6:27–36)

The attitude of a kingdom believer is clear: love and do good to all. Even to our enemies. To live like this is to be like Jesus, and that is the purpose God has for all of his children (Rom. 8:29–30). And it is, after all, what our Master said.

Facing the Dilemma Head-on

When we look squarely at the commands of Jesus, it is no wonder that many Christians have ultimately followed the example of the world and deliberately left love out of their business dealings. "This is just plain impossible. It's hard enough at home or at church. It's impossible in business." So the line goes. "This can't work. You can't love your competitors. You can't even afford to get emotionally attached to your employees. What if you have to let them go or lay them off? And what about negotiations? What about fiercely attacking the market? None of this makes sense!"

Nevertheless, Jesus does not offer us a "duty-free zone" at work in which his commands can be set aside. To put the matter bluntly, we must either embrace Jesus' command to love in business or reject it—and to reject his command is to reject his rule.

Debunking common perceptions of love. The first thing we must do if we are committed to being faithful to Christ in every aspect of our lives is to make sure we are not operating under false concepts. In no area is this more common than in the understanding of what biblical love really is.

For most people, believers and unbelievers alike, love is often characterized as a weak, weepy sort of emotional mush that renders the lover a passive doormat in life. Even if we know better, we still tend to think of love as having pleasant feelings toward someone or by letting people walk all over us. This misconception, generated more by Hollywood than by Scripture, leaves us believing that love must be restricted to the softer circles of life with no place in the heat of battle or business.

How can a man be loving and yet strong? How can a woman love her husband and yet leave him because of abuse? How can a general love his troops (as did Robert E. Lee) and yet lead them into certain death? How can a CEO love an employee that she must terminate for embezzlement? The common misconception of love would lead us to say that he or she cannot and that therefore love cannot work in business—or frankly in any real-life arena.

Grasping the truth about love. Thankfully along with giving us his command to love, Jesus did not leave us without the means of understanding the real meaning of love. Through Scripture and by his example, we can quickly dispel general ignorance and arrive at a definition of love that not only works in the business world but also works better than any other single force.

One of the problems in understanding love is that in our English language we have only one word for "love." We use it in a variety of settings. We love God. We love our family. We love baseball. We love to work. And we love pizza. Now clearly we don't mean that we relate to all these persons and entities in the same way. We differentiate between meanings by context, and we all understand. We are devoted to God. We put the needs of our families above our own. We get excited at a baseball game. We are energized by the challenge of work. And pizza tastes good.

The language of the Bible, however, is much more exact. In fact, there are seven different Greek words used for love in the New Testament. It's as if God really wanted to make this clear. For example, there is a word specifically for the kind of romantic and sexual love shared by a man and a woman (*eros*). There is also a specific word for the bond of friendship and human-to-human caring (*phileo*). And when it comes to the word Jesus used in his various commands, there is one of the most exact words ever penned—*agape*. This word, *agape*, has nothing whatsoever to do with the other words and certainly has no relationship to the namby-pamby definitions generally espoused by the world or the church. It is a strong word, an active word. It is a word that describes an attitude that could come only from the strongest of men and the bravest of women. It is not weak; it is not mushy. It is powerful and world changing. Put simply, the word *agape* speaks of an inward attitude that selflessly puts the needs of others ahead of our own and then acts out in sacrificial service to help them meet their needs. Now where is the weakness in that?

Then there is the example of Jesus himself. Jesus walked in love 24/7. There was no moment in which he did not live in the same agape love in which he commanded us to walk. Yes, he was walking in love when he welcomed little children or when he rescued an adulterous woman from stoning. But he was also walking in love when he stood up to the Pharisees, cleansed the temple, and faced the high priest in his sham trial. In any of these scenarios he could have annihilated his opposition and been thoroughly righteous in doing so, but he chose a different, better response—the response of love. He stood his ground. He spoke the truth. He defended the weak. He reorganized the temple. This is real love in action. It is strong, decisive, fearless, and unstoppable. And what about the Cross? In love, Jesus put the needs of the world above his own and acted sacrificially to meet those needs in the bravest and most honorable act of all time! Weakness? Strength!

So now we are equipped with a more accurate understanding of love. Love does not mean "never having to say you're sorry." Love means being like Jesus. It means dethroning yourself and acting for the best interest of others. It means doing powerful things that powerfully impact those around us and the society in which we live—for their good and for the glory of God.

Applying Love in Business

So how does all this apply to business? Think of the definition and example we have seen. Then let your imagination run free. A man or woman who applied love in business would be the leader who wasn't out for him or herself. Loving in business would provide the only source of real courage for speaking the truth to the board or to a non-performing salesperson. Love would require leaders to keep a constant vigil in terms of what is best for the company or for the client—not what is best for themselves.

- Would love confront nonperformance? Yes!
- Would love strive to offer a better solution than the competition? Yes!
- Would love build a great organization? Yes!
- Would love create a culture that attracted top talent? Yes!
- Would love deal ethically in all situations? Yes!
- Would love produce leaders who never had to remember their lies? Yes!

- Would love lead to a company that investors could trust? Yes!

The list goes on. The point is clear. Once we understand the biblical concept of love, we can see that there is no need to leave it at the office door or in the parking lot. Leave the mushy, sentimental, "everything's OK" drivel outside; it's not love anyway. But throw open the door wide and dare to be obedient to Christ fully in business. Love!

Conclusion

As much as I hate to disagree with my old mentor, the truth is that business and love do go together. There is no need for a dichotomy; there is no separation required. On the contrary, true biblical love will work better and more powerfully in business than any other practice we could devise on our own, and since it's Christ's command, to practice love in business aligns us squarely with our Master's purpose and his power.

7

HR: VALUING PEOPLE AS GOD DOES

It wasn't the first time my wife and I went without a pay-check, and it wouldn't be the last. However, the staff received theirs and never knew of the financial crisis. As the CEO, I had the right to be paid. I had earned my money just as everyone else had. But a choice had to be made, and recognizing that the employees were placed under our care, we decided to ensure that they were paid no matter what happened to us.

An observer doesn't need to look very far into the business world to find issues and conflicts between co-regents and their employers, employers and their employees, management and labor, companies and unions, departments and departments, and, of course, individuals and individuals. In fact, conflict and mistreatment are so common that many look on business as innately corrupt and dehumanizing. The problem is not business, however, but with the people (people like us) in business who refuse to view and value people as God does.

Over the years, the business department designated to oversee people matters has gone through a series of name changes. First it was Payroll, then Personnel, now Human Resources, and in some companies, Human Capital Management. However, with all the name changes, the leopard has not changed its spots. Fundamentally, people are viewed not as assets but as liabilities or tools of production. One only has to witness massive layoffs for the purpose of enhancing stock prices to see just how much the corporate world "values" its employees.

In stark contrast, kingdom-business professionals stand out as men and women deeply committed not only to God's purposes in the world but also to God's values and perspectives. Consequently, they adopt God's estimation of the people around them and adjust their businesses to God's standard rather than adjusting God's standard to their businesses. Consider Isaiah's prophetic message: "'For my thoughts are not your thoughts, neither are your ways my ways,' declares the LORD. 'As the heavens are higher than the earth, so are my ways higher than your ways and my thoughts than your thoughts'" (Isa. 55:8–9). God's ways are different and better. Our challenge as Christians is to adopt them in totality. This is true in all areas of life, but it is especially true in the realm of business, where the temptation to think and act as the world is perhaps stronger than any other area. Specifically, this will require us to learn to think as God does about people and then to treat them as God desires.

Developing the Proper Thoughts about People

The first step in developing a true kingdom perspective on human resource management is to make certain we think rightly about people. If, as the world does, we view people as tools, mere employees, or disposable persons, we will never be able to build a proper HR foundation. Ideas have consequences. We must know and embrace God's perspective on people. We must go to his Word and discover what he thinks and how he feels about people. Then, guided by his thoughts, we can begin to adjust our thinking to his.

A friend of mine rose rapidly to become the first female senior vice president in a major manufacturing company. However, it was not long until Debbie became disillusioned with the attitudes she encountered among other senior executives toward employees. The final straw came when a young MBA-educated consultant appeared in her office with a spreadsheet that he said told him they had to lay off fifty-five people. Debbie refused, resigned, and is now a coach to other aspiring female business leaders. Debbie has a different view of people.

A brief survey of biblical anthropology, the study of humanity, will be helpful to start us on our journey toward thinking of people as God does.

People are the good creation of God. Genesis 1:27 begins with the words, "So God created man," and while to Christians this may seem elementary, the ramifications of this truth are profound. Let the record show that God made man, male and female. We are his creation, his handiwork. We are not evolved apes or scientific accidents or descendants of some amoeba that crawled out of the so-called primordial soup. God made us! That gives each of us a great dignity.

Moreover, when God completed the work of making the human race, he looked on and saw that "it was very good" (Gen. 1:31). At the end of all the other days of creation recorded in Genesis, we read, "God saw that it was good." But when he finished with humanity, when he looked on Adam and Eve, the Bible declares that it was *very* good. In other words, humanity thoroughly pleased God and he looked on it with delight.

Do we look on God's creation with delight? When we think of those who work for us or with us, do we see men and women made by God? Or do we see people who are necessary, useful, but somewhat less than us? I've known many managers over the years who might agree with this idea in theory, but in reality, as they put it, "Humanity is great. It's people I can't stand."

People are created in the image of God. Genesis 1:27 continues with a vital clarification about humanity. It says, "God created man in his own image." The preceding verse gives another phrase, "in our [the Trinity's] likeness." In other words, men and women are not simply another work of art created by the Great Artist to be thought of as any other animal or as part of the environment. Humanity is the crowning achievement of the Creator and was made as his representative, made like him.

It is not my purpose to give a definitive theology of how we are "like God." Volumes exist on this subject, and I can only recommend the study of a good systematic theology for more in-depth consideration. It is enough for our purpose to say that the reference is not to physical likeness, since God has no physical form, nor is it, as some cults teach, a reference to our being little gods. Instead, it means that like God, we have certain characteristics, such as mind, emotion, will, morality, and creativity, that set us apart from the rest of creation.

This is really astounding to think about and flies in the face of the dehumanizing philosophy of the secular world. We are like God. We are made in his image. We therefore have great dignity, indeed, greater dignity than all the rest of creation.

Do we look on those around us as the likeness of God? When we consider our employees, or any other person for that matter, are we impressed with their dignity? Many companies today, both kingdom and secular, have a value statement that in some way calls for treating all employees with dignity and respect. My question is this: How can we treat people with dignity and respect if we don't first think of them as dignified? To stop and remember that this person sitting across the desk from me is made in the image of God profoundly impacts how I treat him or her.

People are the highest point of God's creation. Being created in the image of God puts us in the highest position of all created beings. No other creature even comes close. This very thought astounded King David as he looked into the stars, and it led him to write these beautiful words:

> O LORD, our Lord,
>   how majestic is your name in all the earth!
> You have set your glory
>   above the heavens.
> From the lips of children and infants

>you have ordained praise
>
>   because of your enemies,
>
>   to silence the foe and the avenger.
>
>When I consider your heavens,
>
>   the work of your fingers,
>
>the moon and the stars,
>
>   which you have set in place,
>
>what is man that you are mindful of him,
>
>   the son of man that you care for him?
>
>You made him a little lower than the heavenly beings
>
>   and crowned him with glory and honor.
>
>You made him ruler over the works of your hands;
>
>   you put everything under his feet:
>
>all flocks and herds,
>
>   and the beasts of the field,
>
>the birds of the air,
>
>   and the fish of the sea,
>
>   all that swim the paths of the seas.
>
>O Lord, our Lord,
>
>   how majestic is your name in all the earth! (Ps. 8)

Do we think of people this way? If we don't think of people as they really are, as God's Word says they are, our ability to treat them as he desires is weakened, at best, and destroyed, at worst.

Take for example an older fellow who works for me. Martin is bright and, in his subject, very competent. But he struggles with communication, especially in verbal presentation—to me or to a group. My natural inclination, being a good communicator myself, is to become very impatient and frustrated with Martin. However, when I stop and remind myself that Martin is a creation of God and, in fact, ranks with the very highest of all God's creations, I find myself calmer and able to think of ways to draw out his greatness rather than criticize his weakness.

People are fallen and in rebellion against God. Adam and Eve violated the one command of God in the Garden of Eden and asserted their independence from God on the mistaken belief that since they were honored above all created beings, they were also divine. Accepting Satan's temptation (see Gen. 3), they not only wanted to be the highest creation but also equal to the Creator himself. They threw off his authority and his command, and the results have been disastrous for the entire human race. Sin, disease, war, corruption, and environmental destruction—all spring from this misunderstanding of man's place in the universe.

Moreover, the very nature of humanity changed with that rebellion. Instead of being "very good" and in fellowship with God, Adam and Eve had hearts that became darkened and fallen. The guilty pair also became the selfish pair, the greedy pair, the shamed pair; and all of their descendants were born into estrangement from God.

Nevertheless, while our nature was changed in the Fall, we are still God's creatures, made in his image and still occupying the highest place in creation. We are still the king of all created beings and things, despite the fact that our kingdom is in ruins.

Do we as Christians hold a lower view of humanity because of sin, or do we recognize humanity for what it is? It would be easy for someone to argue at this point that it is foolish to think well of men and women and to treat them accordingly when they have a fallen nature. Shouldn't we view employees as intrinsically lazy, dishonest, and selfish? Shouldn't we think of them realistically? To that I say: Realistically, yes! Harshly, no! Did Jesus think meanly of people because he understood better than anyone else exactly what their condition was? Of course not. The truth is that even as Jesus looked on fallen individuals and saw them for what they were, he still loved them and understood them to be wonderful examples of God's creative grace—fallen but redeemable!

One of my favorite stories about Jesus is the account of how he met with and embraced Zacchaeus (see Luke 19:1–9). I remember this story from childhood. Zacchaeus was a tax collector who cheated the people of Israel even as he served the occupying government of Rome. When Zacchaeus heard that Jesus was coming to his city, he climbed up a tree to be able to catch a glimpse of him as he walked by. However, when Jesus saw Zacchaeus up in the tree, he immediately called him down and ended up staying as a guest at his house—an encounter that led to Zacchaeus's salvation. Most people hated Zacchaeus; Jesus valued him and treated him accordingly.

People are redeemed at a great price. To be redeemed means to be bought or liberated at a price. We as Christians recognize that one of the major themes of the entire Bible is the "redemption story," the message that God was willing to sacrifice his Son in order to bring fallen creatures back into a vital and eternal relationship with him.

There is a great lesson for us in this in terms of how to think of people as well. Here's the principle: the price paid indicates an estimate of value. In other words, the value we place on an object is indicated by the price we are willing to pay to own it. This is true in basic economics, and it is especially true in the divine economics of salvation. If you want to understand the value that God places on the human race, look at the price he paid to free us from the bondage of sin and to place us into the kingdom: the blood of Christ. The apostle Peter put it this way, "For you know that it was not with perishable things such as silver or gold that you were redeemed from the empty way of life handed down to you from your forefathers, but with the precious blood of Christ, a lamb without blemish or defect" (1 Pet. 1:18–19). Incredible! God was willing to give his Son for us.

Do we value others in this way? Once, while attending a meeting, I heard the CEO of a large company say with great feeling, "He's worthless!" When he caught the look on my face, he immediately adjusted his statement by adding, "I mean in terms of business." The truth is, Edward said exactly what he meant and felt the first time. In his view, the employee we were discussing had no value, no worth; he was worthless. Sadly, this attitude pervaded most of Edward's dealings with those who worked for his company, and over time, it became a very hard place to work. How differently would people have felt about Edward's company if Edward had felt differently about them? We are not worthless; we are of great worth to God and should be recognized as such.

People will share in God's kingdom. Finally, in our brief survey of the Bible's teaching about humanity, we discover that God's intent is for those who embrace his offer of redemption to join him in ruling the universe. Regardless of the particular brand of eschatology (the study of the end times) one embraces, these words reveal how God views our future role. Singing to the glorified Christ, the inhabitants of heaven proclaim: "You are worthy to take the scroll and to open its seals, because you were slain, and with your blood you purchased men for God from every tribe and language and people and nation. *You have made them to be a kingdom and priests to serve our God, and they will reign on the earth*" (Rev. 5:9–10, emphasis added).

Is this how we view the people who work for us? We struggle to see them advancing to the next level in the warehouse or on the shop floor. We find it hard to imagine them promoted. God, on the other hand, has destined them for a co-regent position in his kingdom!

In this brief survey, I have wanted only to demonstrate how God thinks of people and to ask whether we view them the same way. To the degree we comply with God's thoughts, we will be able to move toward the proper actions those thoughts require; to the degree we still think differently than God thinks, we will find the next section very difficult, since proper treatment requires proper thought.

Practicing the Proper Treatment of People

At our home in the North Carolina mountains, which my wife has turned into a wonderful bed-and-breakfast inn, we have many beautiful antiques. They are quite valuable and rare. My wife spent a great deal of time collecting them and spent a great deal of money paying for them. How do you think we treat them? We treat them according to the value we place on them. We protect them. We quickly remove glasses others have set on them. We avoid bumping them or scratching them. We treat them according to our estimation of their worth. The same is true with people, with our employees. If you and I value them as God does, we will strive to treat them as God does. Specifically, we will…

Provide for them. One of the main reasons God calls us into business is to create enterprises through which men and women may work and have their physical needs met, as well as use their own abundance to meet the needs of others (see Eph. 4:28). Contrary to common belief, work is not the result of the Fall or the result of God's curse. Reading in context, we can see in Genesis 3:17–19 that it is not work that God introduces as a curse—it is fruitless work and frustrating toil. Work is not the hard part; the hard part is working in an environment that once cooperated but now resists our labors. In chapter 1 we discussed how the creation mandate given by God to Adam and Eve before the Fall provides a foundational theology of work as part of God's original good plan (see Gen. 1:26–31). God intends for us to work to provide for ourselves, and he intends for business to provide opportunities for productive work. That is why most of our three hundred graduates overseas have as a major part of their kingdom impact statement the responsibility to provide employment for their unemployed brothers and sisters.

Business is not charity; it is a means of provision through labor. Essentially, from biblical times men and women have exchanged their labor and their sweat for food, shelter, and money; this is exactly what God had in mind. Jesus himself said to his disciples, "The worker deserves his wages" (Luke 10:7). The exchange should be fair—a fair day's work for a fair day's pay. It should be paid on time—"Withhold not good from them to whom it is due, when it is in the power of thine hand to do *it*" (Prov. 3:27 KJV).

But the concept of provision is greater than just paying wages. It casts business owners in the role of stewards who are responsible for those placed in their care. Our employees are our responsibility under God, and as servant leaders, we should constantly be thinking of how we can care for them and for their needs.

Boaz, the rich landowner in the book of Ruth, exemplifies this kind of concern when, observing the poor widow Ruth gleaning on his land, he instructs his field hands to leave some grain in the field for Ruth to pick up. Later in the story, Ruth appeals to Boaz for protection, and he signifies his agreement by spreading his cloak over her as a covering. Technically Boaz is not Ruth's employer, but he does serve to demonstrate the kind of attitude today's employers should have—to look out for the needs of their employees.

My largest client has over six hundred employees. Often when we meet for strategic planning or other management discussions, I note that the CEO speaks of concern for the possible impact his decisions will have on the company's workers: on their income, job security, or benefits. This concern is at the core of his leadership and reflects a biblical attitude toward human resources.

Respect them. "Get out of my face!" screamed the president. "I don't want to hear this anymore!" The vice president of human resources had just brought a particularly sticky concern to her boss. An employee was being mistreated and abused—verbally and financially. Instead of finding a sympathetic ear or a concerned response, Helen was treated with the same disrespect that created the problem in the first place. Any idea where the problem originated? It started in the president's office.

If the men and women who work for us are created in the image of God and redeemed by the blood of Christ, we should treat them with respect. How often cruelty and condescension characterize the treatment of and communication with employees. Contrast that with the respectful treatment of individuals by the Lord Jesus. Seeing people for what they truly were led the Savior to speak to them and to manage them accordingly. The Gospels are filled with examples of this, but none is more powerful than John's account of Jesus' meeting with the woman caught in adultery (see John 8:1–11). This wonderful story illustrates how respect can transform a life. The woman was guilty. Jesus knew it and she knew it. That was never even discussed. Instead, with compassion that recognized the inherent dignity of the woman, Jesus first protected her and then restored her. "Where are they?" he asked. "Has no one condemned you?" "No one, sir," she replied. "Then neither do I condemn you…. Go now and leave your life of sin" (John 8:10–11).

Give them clear expectations and appropriate consequences. As a consultant to management in various parts of the world, I hear one consistent complaint from employees— that they are never sure what is actually expected of them in their work. As employers, we owe it to our workers to make our expectations clear and specific. Consider God's treatment of Israel with clear and specific commands. Consider Micah's summary of God's expectations: "He has showed you, O man, what is good. And what does the LORD require of you? To act justly and to love mercy and to walk humbly with your God" (Mic. 6:8). God has not left us to guess. He has made his desires abundantly clear—so that we are without excuse. In the same way, Christian employers can follow God's example and make job expectations and requirements clear beyond all misunderstanding.

Moreover, when expectations are clear, it is easy to apply appropriate consequences—both positive (reward) and negative (discipline). As an example of this kind of thinking, examine Deuteronomy 28; here the Lord completes the review and renewal of his covenant with Israel by telling them exactly what they can expect if they meet his requirements and if they do not. The situation is this. The Israelites are on the edge of entering the Promised Land, and Moses gathers them together and spends twenty-seven chapters reminding them of the laws and statutes that God expected them to live by in their new homeland. "Do not kill." "Do not steal." "Love God with all your heart and soul and mind and strength." These are the performance expectations that God laid down for his people. Then, to complete the model, Moses makes it clear that obedience to God's commands will result in great blessing and reward (Deut. 28:1–14) and that disobedience will lead to terrible suffering and destruction (Deut. 28:15–68).

Jesus' approach in the New Testament is less specific but no less clear. What does he want his followers to do? He wants them to love one another (see John 13:34–35). The result of obedience to this command is twofold: a strong testimony to the world (v. 35) and greater intimacy with the Father (see John 14:21). The result of disobedience is implied but forceful—the world will ridicule Christ, and we will not experience closeness to God.

How does this work out practically in business? On a corporate level I would make one of my first priorities to establish a Performance

Management System—a program of clear expectations, feedback or coaching, and rewards or consequences. Any good consultant can help you create and implement such a system, and the resulting increase in morale and performance will more than pay for the cost of such an initiative. On an individual level, how clearly do your employees know your expectations? Ask them and listen to see whether what they think you want is what you really want. Then commit to a program of personal interaction with them—coaching them regularly to improve and rewarding or reprimanding them for their specific performance. The level of trust, confidence, and openness that will develop in your company will amaze you.

Protect them. The Lord commits himself to the protection of his people. He says so in Isaiah: "Even to your old age and gray hairs I am he, I am he who will sustain you. I have made you and I will carry you; I will sustain you and I will rescue you" (Isa. 46:4). In the same way, as employers we should spend time thinking and praying about how we can protect our workers rather than merely focusing on how we can get more production from them or do without so many of them. Our decisions, which are guided by our attitudes, have the potential to shield our employees from unemployment, accidents, harassment, and many other dangers present in the marketplace. For example, I know of one company that increased its per diem allowance for travel to give employees enough money to stay in hotels with indoor hallways as opposed to cheaper motels with outdoor room entrances. Its concern was employee safety—especially that of its female employees—on the road. The cost was incidental, the company felt, in comparison to the human cost of an assaulted worker.

In a less dramatic move, another company I work with provides airline club memberships to its frequent travelers so that they can get out of the crowds at the airport and relax before a flight. This "protection" allows them to feel valued, to get more work done, and to arrive at their destination a little less frazzled. It doesn't always have to cost a lot of money to provide a bit of protection.

Develop and nurture them. Knowing the weaknesses of humanity, Jesus nevertheless focused the majority of his earthly ministry on selecting and developing those who would work for and with him in transforming the earth. In fact, if you examine his ministry, you will discover that his public appearances (sermons, confrontations, miracles, etc.), while dramatic, were rare compared to the time he spent in private prayer and conversation with his small band of disciples.

Many management experts think that hiring is the most important decision any business owner can ever make. Jesus certainly acted as if he agreed spending an entire night in prayer before choosing his inner circle (see Luke 6:12–13). Then, with the fateful decision made, the Lord poured his life into them until the day he was taken from them. We can follow his example by recognizing the important choice in hiring employees and, once they are hired, valuing them and investing time and money to train them and nurture their growth. Indeed, the development of employees, if undertaken in a caring and prayerful way, can be a prime fulfillment of Jesus' command to disciple the nations (see Matt. 28:19). This is one of the major purposes of a kingdom business.

What are specific ways to do this? In addition to traditional training seminars, consider the following ideas. Hire an executive coach for emerging leaders. Select a small group of employees to meet with regularly for discussion about business, your business, and about life. Take employees with you when you travel and let them see you interact with customers, competitors, and others. In short, more than teaching, involve them in your life as Jesus involves us in his.

Listen to them. As God's ear is ever open to our cries, so our ears can be constantly open to listen to our employees. Common sense and common decency demand this. However, our standard is God, and if we view people as he does, we will value them enough to invest time in hearing and responding to what they have to say. A verse that every kingdom employer should memorize and apply is James 1:19: "Everyone should be quick to listen, slow to speak."

Many companies, kingdom and secular, provide opportunities for communication such as employee surveys, employee focus groups, and breakfast-with-the-CEO programs. However you choose to do it, do it. Verne Harnish, author of *Mastering the Rockefeller Habits*, developed an innovative approach. He advocates creating an e-mail address called hassles@[yourcompany].com. Employees can e-mail you with things that frustrate them. Whatever you do, listen. And in your heart make sure that you really want to listen.

Speak the truth to them. When we do speak, we must speak truth. Jesus always did—even when the truth would challenge and convict others or bring harm to him. In fact, Jesus identified himself as *being* the Truth (see John 14:6). Love speaks the truth and never has to waffle or "spin." As Paul told the Ephesians, we should determine to "speak the truth in love" (Eph. 4:15; see also Eph. 4:25).

One of my clients (not a kingdom company but in many ways run by biblical principles) has, as one of its core values, the virtue "honesty." I have seen them live up to this on more than one occasion, and the fruit of trust among employees is astounding. Recently, a valued employee's role was being eliminated. Rather than beat around the bush and try to spin the situation, the man's manager, Jill, simply laid it out there. Essentially Jill told the man the history of how the situation came to be and that there simply was no role in the future for him. I was on the call when Jill explained all this. With great care and respect, Jill offered a very honorable exit plan that the employee accepted. I was amazed at the maturity of the conversation compared with the more emotional calls I am usually called on to assist with. The next day Jill received a sincere thank you e-mail from the now-former employee that reciprocated the respect with which he had been treated.

Get to know them. In his excellent book *Leadership Is an Art*, Max DuPree tells the story of one of his father's employees—a millwright. While attending the man's funeral, DuPree was impressed with poetry that was read at the service. He asked the man's widow who wrote it. "He did," she replied. DuPree walked out humbled and ashamed that all the years he had known the man he had never gotten to know him well enough to discover that in addition to being a skilled craftsman he was a poet!

The essence of the Christian life is that God calls us to know him and to have a deeply personal relationship with him (see John 17:3;

1 Cor. 1:9). If God cares enough for us to invite us into a relationship with him, can we not follow his example and get to know our employees in a more personal way?

Conclusion

The preceding sections all describe ways in which God, our Creator-Father, expresses his valuing of us. What better model to follow than his?

Here's a practical suggestion. Create a survey based on the criteria previously discussed and dare to ask your employees how they feel you are doing in each area. Then take the results and set yourself to improve in each area.

True human-resource management begins with thinking God's thoughts. We must learn to see people as God sees them and to turn those thoughts into practical actions in terms of the way we treat those around us and those who work for us. Only in this way can we fulfill the relational requirements of being a kingdom business.

8

SERVANT LEADERSHIP: THE VITAL RELATIONSHIP

Seeing the founder and CEO in the kitchen was unusual, to say the least. While the employees sat in the conference, he cheerfully unpacked the groceries, set out the food, and prepared the meal they would later enjoy. "How could this be leadership?" some wondered. "He's the boss."

In his excellent book *Good to Great,* business author Jim Collins describes the characteristics of companies that have gone beyond being good at what they do to being great. One of those characteristics is what he calls "Level 5 Leadership." His premise, based on significant research, is that great companies have great leadership—but not the kind of leadership you might imagine. In fact, Collins's work demonstrates that the charismatic, celebrity leader often turns out to be ineffective over the long term; the same is true of the driven, taskmaster leader. What works, what builds great companies, is leaders who consistently put the good of the organization above their own interests, who are willing to make the hard decisions, even when it hurts, and who practice humility in letting others take the credit for a job well done. As I read *Good to Great,* I was amazed at how closely this model of leadership parallels the servant leadership that Jesus exemplified and taught; I was even more amazed to see that Collins, after outlining this marvelous model of leadership, stringently denies that he is talking about servant leadership. His reason for this denial, I believe, is due to a basic misunderstanding of what true servant leadership is.

For many, the concept of servant leadership is about weakness and passivity. The world simply cannot comprehend a model of leadership that is not about power and the exercise of it. To many, leadership is only about control and results; this requires the gaining of power. Servant leadership, they argue, is the antithesis of this and, therefore, cannot work. They are wrong.

The ultimate leader, and consequently the ultimate example of leadership, is Jesus Christ. After all, his title is KING OF KINGS and LORD OF LORDS—the leader's leader. Jesus possesses all power and authority (see Matt. 28:18). His physical, mental, emotional, and spiritual leadership is unparalleled in human experience, as is his impact on world history. Yet Jesus described his style of leadership, his philosophy of leadership, as that of a servant. In fact, he himself said, "I am among you as one who *serves*" (Luke 22:27, emphasis added). Clearly, whatever servant leadership means, it does not mean weakness or ineffectiveness.

It is this concept of servant leadership that Jesus calls us to imitate. As business leaders, we are to be servant business leaders. Nowhere is the Master's view on leadership and servanthood expressed more clearly than in the following passage. James and John, two of Jesus' disciples, come to him with a bold request. "Make us great," they demand. In response, Jesus teaches them (and us) the true meaning of greatness, honor, and leadership.

> James and John, Zebedee's sons, came up to him. "Teacher, we have something we want you to do for us."
>
> "What is it? I'll see what I can do."
>
> "Arrange it," they said, "so that we will be awarded the highest places of honor in your glory—one of us at your right, the other at your left."

Jesus said, "You have no idea what you're asking. Are you capable of drinking the cup I drink, of being baptized in the baptism I'm about to be plunged into?"

"Sure," they said. "Why not?"

Jesus said, "Come to think of it, you *will* drink the cup I drink, and be baptized in my baptism. But as to awarding places of honor, that's not my business. There are other arrangements for that."

When the other ten heard of this conversation, they lost their tempers with James and John. Jesus got them together to settle things down. "You've observed how godless rulers throw their weight around," he said, "and when people get a little power how quickly it goes to their heads. It's not going to be that way with you. Whoever wants to be great must become a servant. Whoever wants to be first among you must be your slave. That is what the Son of Man has done: He came to serve, not to be served—and then to give away his life in exchange for many who are held hostage." (Mark 10:35–45, MSG)

What a powerful contrast. James and John expressed clearly how the world thinks of leadership—greatness, honor, power, authority, control. In fairness to the two of them, the rest of the group also thought this way; notice how angry the others were at the request (v. 41). It is as if they would lose something if Jesus granted what James and John wanted. Jesus, on the other hand, with a clear rebuke to all of the Twelve, explains that the way the world thinks of leadership will not work in his kingdom; he expects leaders to become great by serving.

The World's View of Leadership

In 1 John 2:15–16, the apostle warns followers of Jesus, "Do not love the world or anything in the world." He then explains what "the world" is all about—"the cravings of sinful man, the lust of his eyes and the boasting of what he has and does." In simple terms, the world is a system of thought and action characterized by three things: the acquisition of pleasure, the accumulation of possessions, and the achievement of position. Put even more bluntly: *The world is all about me! I am the center of it and the purpose of it. I live to experience my pleasure. I work to build my wealth. I ascend to gain mastery over others.*

Beneath all of this pursuit is the underlying belief that these things are what matter and what make life worth living. People all over the world believe this. They have always believed this. That is why they do what they do. And to live this "life" to the fullest requires power.

A great deal of power resides in business. And that's another reason unredeemed business has gotten such a reputation for being corrupt and evil—it is the ultimate means of achieving what selfish men and women believe makes life count!

As a result of this faulty way of thinking, people have sacrificed without measure to attain power and then, once gained, they exercise this power to satisfy their worldly desires, regardless of the consequences. One only has to examine the headlines about Tyco, Enron, and WorldCom to see both the greed and its consequences.

Think for a moment about those the world considers great. What do they experience? Abundant pleasure. What do they have? Wealth. What do they do? They exercise authority over others. This, then, is the measure of greatness—the person with the "most for me" wins and is counted the greatest of all. Held in check only by external means (laws, societal norms, etc.) they walk just one slippery step away from the precipice of unbridled self-centeredness. And we call that leadership!

The Kingdom View of Leadership and Greatness

The kingdom of Jesus turns the world on its head. It sets everything upside down from an earthly perspective but right side up from God's viewpoint. Jesus, the ultimate cosmic revolutionary, goes to the very heart of our quest for greatness and leadership; he both speaks and lives the leadership of God. And it is to this form of leadership that the true kingdom professional must aspire.

In the dispute between his disciples in Mark 10, Jesus immediately perceives that his followers are arguing over greatness based on the world's definition. The ambition of James and John (or that of the other disciples) is frankly no different from the unregenerate world. They want greatness—which to them means to sit with Christ in a position of power, authority, possession, and pleasure. Their misconception, if left uncorrected, would lead to a full-scale devolution of the kingdom Jesus came to establish. Indeed, the entire future of the kingdom rested on his followers understanding and embracing a radical new view of what leadership and greatness is. To be great, says Jesus, is to be a servant and to lead as he did. Surely, this is not what James and John were thinking!

If the world says that life is about gaining power, Jesus says that in his kingdom it is about giving power away. If, according to human reasoning, it is about experiencing pleasure, then, according to Christ, it is about providing support. If it is about the exercise of authority and having people obey, Jesus' kingdom worldview demands that this authority be exercised with the heart of a slave whose only interest is the welfare of those whom he or she is privileged to serve. The measure of success is not what we gain but what we give, not who serves us but whom we serve.

It is an indication of our fallenness and the degree to which we have accepted the world's philosophy of leadership when we find ourselves responding to this perspective with the question, "How can this possibly work in business?" Our objection is our indictment! Yet even in secular business, Collins has documented that leaders who genuinely put the welfare of the organization and its employees ahead of their own interests achieve superior results. Despite objections to the contrary, Collins has observed true servant leadership in action. He has cataloged those who empower others rather than seek to gain power, those who make hard and personally costly decisions because of the benefit to those entrusted to their care. He has discovered individuals who have thrown aside the quest for glory and allowed others to be praised in their stead. And in his study, Collins has discovered the point that Jesus was making.

The Application of Servant Leadership

We will search in vain for a checklist of activities that make up servant leadership. True kingdom leadership is not so much a matter of practice as a matter of personal character. We see servant leadership in practice, but that is not where it comes from; it comes from the heart. I recall being interviewed for a Christian magazine, and when I was asked what steps a person could take to become a servant leader, I totally confounded the interviewer by telling her that there were no steps, only the change that Christ works in our hearts that we then live out through the Holy Spirit. Therefore, since it is a matter of character, we must look elsewhere—to the heart and those areas of life most closely connected to it. Can you say, "In my heart, I am a servant; I think like a servant, and therefore I lead like one"? I suggest the following questions as a means of self-examination.

What is the attitude of my heart toward others? How do I think and feel about those I lead? What are my motivations in working as hard as I do or in demanding high levels of performance in others? What am I trying to achieve? What will I gain from all of this? Are others more important to me than I am to myself? Am I expecting others to work while I play? How do I keep score—through income and possessions or through impact on others?

To whom am I accountable? "The heart is deceitful above all things and beyond cure. Who can understand it?" (Jer. 17:9). Because of this reality, I cannot trust my own self-examination or my personal diagnosis of the condition of my heart. I need accountability—men around me (or women if you are a woman) to whom I must give account and to whom I have given permission to press into the inner recesses of my soul. *Where are those men, those women, in my life?*

To think that you will safely navigate the waters from worldly leadership to servant leadership without the assistance of others is foolish and will only lead to self-deception (a skill deftly learned by most leaders). Nevertheless, I find few business leaders who actively participate in any type of accountability group.

One of my best friends is the leader of a group known as TEC, or The Executive Committee. TEC groups are monthly gatherings of CEOs and company presidents for the purpose of learning, encouragement, counsel, and accountability. In the Christian world this same model is beginning to spring up in forums like Buck Jacobs's C12 groups, Ray Miller's Trac 3 meetings, and ISI (Iron Sharpening Iron) groups.

What do my employees tell me? When was the last time I sincerely asked my employees how I might serve them and facilitate their success? Have I honestly sought "360-degree feedback"? Warning—we can't be surprised if our employees respond to us with suspicion when we ask them for their input. Their model of leadership is from the world as well.

What is my earning power compared to that of my employees? Jesus taught that our treasure and our hearts are closely aligned. *Is my practice with money—how much for me compared to how much for my employees—a positive indicator of the deeper attitudes of my inner self?* I'm not suggesting some socialist, share-the-wealth program, nor am I saying that a business owner should not receive a higher income than an entry-level worker. What we should look for here is how much higher our income is than that of the rest of the company.

These are just a few of the questions a sincere kingdom professional will want to ask from time to time. Servant-leadership practices flow from a servant-leadership character, and therefore, it is to the heart we must constantly go. "Search me, O God, and know my heart; test me and know my anxious thoughts. See if there is any offensive way in me, and lead me in the way everlasting" (Ps. 139:23–24).

The Impact Potential of Servant Leaders in Business

As a business owner, I often think of a story that is the record of what happened when Rehoboam, the son of King Solomon, took over the throne. The account is in 1 Kings 12, and I would strongly recommend that anyone desiring to lead as a servant read it regularly. Here's what happened. Rehoboam came to power after the death of his father and was immediately approached by the people of Israel to hear words from his heart. What kind of leader would he be? Would he be fair? Would he be just? Would he lighten their load and look after their interests, or would he continue the hard service that had set in during the last years of Solomon's life? Rehoboam listened to the people and asked for time to consider his answer. He then privately sought counsel from his court advisors. There was quite a divide in the advice he received. Older, wiser, and experienced counselors urged him to heed the concerns of the people and to lead as a servant. They said, "If today you will be a servant to these people and serve them and give them a favorable answer, they will always be your servants" (1 Kings 12:7). However, the younger advisors, clearly embracing the world's view of leadership, convinced Rehoboam to come out "strong" and to show the people who was boss. Following the advice of these worldly counselors, Rehoboam chose the path of fallen, self-centered leadership and determined to use the people as a means of enhancing his own prestige and power. His exact words reveal something of the attitude and arrogance of his heart. "My father made your yoke heavy; I will make it even heavier," he said. "My father scourged you with whips; I will scourge you with scorpions" (1 Kings 12:14). Is it any wonder that when the people heard his words they renounced their new king and launched a rebellion against him? The ensuing civil war in Israel splintered the nation in such a way that it would never recover its past greatness.

Craig is one of my best friends in the entire world and has been for years. We came to Christ at almost exactly the same time. Craig is a very successful business leader and has learned a great deal about what people are looking for. I remember he once told me that when a new leader comes into an organization, there are three questions the people ask. "Does she know what she's doing? Can I trust her? Does she care about me as a person?" In other words, is this person competent, credible, and caring? If the answer is no to one of these questions, people will have a hard time following; if the answer is no to two of them, they won't follow at all. Clearly, Rehoboam failed the test and reaped the results.

There are many Rehoboams in business today, men and women who put themselves above their employees, who disrespect them, and who reap the harsh fruit of their attitudes and actions. When Emma came to me, she was distraught. "What's happened to my company?" she asked. "It's like the soul has been eaten away." I agreed with her summary and asked her if she really wanted to hear the truth. She did, and so I proceeded to tell her that the change occurred when she hired Sam to be her Number Two. Selfish, rude, harsh, and unethical, Sam had systematically offended, demotivated, humiliated, or driven off practically everyone in the company. He wasn't trusted. He wasn't liked. He dominated; he didn't lead. And the impact of this kind of self-seeking leadership on a company once known for being a truly great place to work was devastating. Good people were simply turned off by poor leadership. To her credit, Emma accepted my input, and the next day she asked Sam to leave. The entire company gave one huge sigh of relief, and before long it was healthy and growing again.

On the other hand, consider the impact of eleven men who had learned what servant leadership meant at the feet of the ultimate Servant Leader. Peter, James, John (yes, the very ones who argued over greatness earlier), and others allowed the Holy Spirit to work in their inner beings and to establish the character of Jesus himself within them. They put Christ's interests above their own—embracing poverty and suffering for his name's sake. They sacrificed all claim to worldly possessions—giving up houses and lands, abandoning their own careers to follow him. They, who once raged at each other over their relative positions in the kingdom, refused to debate over position or prestige; even Peter, arguably the chief apostle, referred to himself as just another elder (see 1 Pet. 5:1). They consistently abandoned the easier path in order to bring blessing to the church. And as a result of their lives and their ministries, countless millions have come into a living relationship with God, and the world has literally been changed for the good!

"Okay," you might say. "I can see this in ministry. What about in business?" I have no idea as to whether Lee Iaccoca claims to be a believer, but I do know that when he was brought back to save Chrysler Motors, he did so for the huge salary of one dollar per year! Arguably he already had plenty of money and didn't need more, but regardless of the reason, where have you ever seen a corporate executive work for no income? The impact of this decision, which was publicized for all the right reasons, was an employee and investor community that respected its leader and genuinely believed that he was there to help save the ailing company.

I've seen the same thing up close and personal. I've worked with Jane and her company for several years. They operate a kingdom company in Asia. Beginning with only a few thousand dollars and a vision, Jane now operates two factories. The majority of her employees have become believers in a country that is officially atheist, and as a group they are always seeking new ways to reach out to the community—providing jobs, education, and housing and even helping people to leave and start their own kingdom businesses. How did all this happen? Apart from the obvious blessing of God, I believe that the success, and the spirit of the company to serve others flows directly from Jane's own servant heart. Without official publication, everyone in the company knows that Jane and her family gave up relative wealth in the United States to move to Asia, that they live on far less than they did in America, and that they regularly give up their salary to help an employee or a member of the community (Christian or not). They exhibit servant leadership, and the world sits up and takes notice.

Another example of servant leadership in business is something I witnessed personally. Tom is one of the most respected CEOs I have ever known. His employees respect and admire him, and the effort they put into building their company together is amazing. How does Tom exhibit servant leadership? I recently heard that when the board refused to authorize additional stock options for employees Tom felt contributed greatly to the success of the company, he had some of his own shares reassigned to them. No wonder his employees are so loyal.

What about us? Will we lead as Rehoboam—thinking our employees exist to make us successful? Or will we, like the apostles, dethrone ourselves and lay aside our self-interest so that the greater good may come?

Conclusion

The greatest of all relationships in the institution of business is the relationship of leader to follower, employer to employee. In that relationship more than any other, we have the opportunity to exhibit supernatural living, to demonstrate the very character of Christ, to live in bold relief to the world's accepted standard of leadership, and to prove to all that there truly is a better way, a kingdom way!

A KINGDOM BUSINESS IS
OPERATIONAL

9

OPERATIONAL EXCELLENCE: THE TRUE PURSUIT

My company and its sister company were founded for micro-enterprise development among the world's poorest and least reached. To date we've seen three hundred kingdom companies begin and remain in operation in nineteen locations around the world. We have been, by all accounts, quite successful. Yet each year we completely revise our process and curriculum. Why? Because we are deeply committed to operational excellence in everything we do.

We have now come to the fourth characteristic of a kingdom business—operational excellence. My hope is that by now we are all convinced of the high calling of God in business (our vocation), are pursuing a better understanding of God's kingdom purpose for our business (our intention), and are seeking to walk as he walked with the people around us in business (our relations). The final focus, Operational Excellence, provides the last pillar on which godly business is based.

Operations refers simply to the how of running a business. I am using the term in its broadest sense to describe all the various functions of business—strategy, HR, financial management, IS, technology, sales, and service. In other words, I am either making something, moving something, selling something, servicing those who buy something, or recording data about something. In all of this, God is to be honored.

Does God really care how we run our businesses so long as we treat people right? Does it matter as long as our hearts are right with God? Yes! It matters how we run our businesses. It matters to God. And it matters to our employees, to our customers, to our suppliers, and to our investors. It matters to those who might be touched through our kingdom impact and purpose. It is not just a matter of testimony or creating more profits to give away. Indeed, if business itself is our calling from God and an integral part of our ministry to and for him, then the way we run it is a vital part of our relationship to him. Our business affairs reflect our heart attitude toward God— and he cares.

Years ago, while I was still in seminary, one of my professors said, "There is no greater sin than to bore people with the Word of God." His point was simple: we should strive for excellence in our preaching. None of us would have much respect for a pastor whose study habits were slovenly, whose sermons were dry and boring, whose discipline was lax, or whose administration of his duties was lazy. Why, if we believe that business is a ministry and calling from God, would we feel any differently about the manner in which we run our companies?

In Search of Excellence

Go to any bookstore, find the business section, and try to count the books. You'll quickly realize that there are too many and give up. Business writing is a multibillion-dollar industry, with new volumes appearing weekly. Some are solid, some are good, but most are nonsense and nothing more than warmed-over ideas from previous authors. Yet there are a few outstanding authors whose works have challenged us to pursue excellence and to gain from the "best management practices" of others. My own favorites include Tom Peters, Jim Collins, Peter Drucker, and Edwards Deming. The reason I like these authors so much is that they have a deep passion for business and for business excellence. They get angry and frustrated over slovenly habits and resting on past success. They push and persuade us to find new and better ways of doing things—to develop stronger strategy, to build better teams, to produce better goods, to utilize information more effectively, to give better service. And they do this, for the most part, without any reference to God. To them, business practice is about living, about beating the competition, about the satisfaction of transforming an industry, and about making a difference. Since it matters so much to them, they cannot endure anything less than doing the best job possible with the resources at their disposal with a view to continuous improvement. How much more should the servants of Christ share the same passion for excellence?

What is ironic about these books is that when you look at them from God's perspective, with a biblical mind-set, you'll find that you still agree with them. Why? Because, for the most part, the principles and practices they embrace and chronicle are directly or indirectly linked to the truth of God's Word. Here are a few examples of these principles and practices:

Developing a core ideology (Jim Collins). Determining what it is that you believe and care about, then building your organization on that foundation, is at the heart of every great company. God originated that idea when he gave Israel the Ten Commandments. This was to be their "core ideology," a summary form of all that God called them to live by and the culture he desired, and they were to build their nation on this foundation. Even putting the core values where they could be readily seen is a biblical idea. Consider the instruction of Moses to the Israelites in Deuteronomy 6, a passage that Jesus referred to on several occasions.

> Hear, O Israel: The LORD our God, the LORD is one. Love the LORD your God with all your heart and with all your soul and with all your strength. These commandments that I give you today are to be upon your hearts. Impress them on your children. Talk about them when you sit at home and when you walk along the road, when you lie down and when you get up.

Tie them as symbols on your hands and bind them on your foreheads. Write them on the doorframes of your houses and on your gates. (vv. 4–9)

Two things stand out from this passage. The first is the command to love God—which both Jesus and Paul identified as the core of all core values to the people of God. The second is that these core values, or core ideology, were to be constantly in front of the people to remind them what mattered and what God desired of them.

Eliminating fear from the workplace (Edwards Deming). Challenges to stop blaming people and to drive fear from the workplace were major tenets of the transformational approach to business espoused by Deming, the man who led Japan's resurgence after World War II and fathered the U.S. quality movement during the 1980s. Fear discourages and stifles innovation; it leads to cover-ups rather than freedom and creativity. Deming knew this and so did the apostle John, who spoke of the effects of fear this way: "There is no fear in love. But perfect loves drives out fear, because fear has to do with punishment" (1 John 4:18). Obviously, John had learned well from his Master who said, "Do not be afraid" (John 14:27).

Set "bigger than life" goals or BHAGS (Jim Collins). A BHAG, or big, hairy, audacious goal, doesn't discourage people; on the contrary, it inspires people to greater achievement. Whether it is the idea of putting a man on the moon and returning him safely to earth (John F. Kennedy), creating an easy-to-use computer (Steve Jobs), or rebuilding the shattered walls around Jerusalem (Nehemiah), there is something in the impossible that reaches into our souls and energizes us. How's this for a BHAG: Go, therefore, and disciple the nations (Matt. 28:19)!

Deliver "Wow!" service (Tom Peters). As early as 1980, Tom Peters was preaching the "service revolution" and recording the examples of such companies as Sewell Village Cadillac in Dallas, a car dealer whose shop floors were reputed to be cleaner than most of our homes. Companies invested millions of dollars in customer-service training, and many reaped great financial rewards through increased customer loyalty. The root of this idea, however, is not found in any business book; rather, it is found in the writings of Paul where he urges believers to put the needs of others ahead of their own (Phil. 2:5–11).

Get the "right people" on the bus (Jim Collins). Collins opens his book on great companies, *Good to Great*, with a chapter on making sure that you have the right people on your team and in the right places before you attempt to create strategy or lead your company. This is sound advice. Jesus did it when he spent an entire night in prayer before choosing the Twelve to whom he would entrust the building of his church (Luke 6:12–16).

I could continue with many more examples, but I am not seeking to catalog every practice of excellence. My point is not to try to prove that every major business idea can be found in Scripture—surely there is nothing about business process reengineering in the Bible. Nor am I seeking to present the Bible as the ultimate business text; it is not. (In fact, I would encourage you to read every good, secular business book you can get your hands on.) Instead, I am suggesting that with a biblical mind-set we can examine the practices that are touted as being the best and discern which ones mesh with the requirements of Scripture. My point is to show that many of the practices of truly excellent companies are consistent with the Bible. Excellence in business corresponds with biblical practice.

How to Build an Excellent Company

To offer up to God anything less than excellence in the way we run our business is to dishonor him. This is a clear application of 1 Corinthians 10:31: "whatever you do, do it all for the glory of God." Moreover, substandard business practices can shrink our profits, throw shadows on our relationships, and retard our ability to fulfill our kingdom purpose. So how do we learn what is excellent, and how do we put it into practice?

Pray. The first step in running an excellent company is to pray. Pray over your company. Pray over your decisions. Pray over hiring and promoting. Pray for growth. Pray for servant hearts. Pray for wisdom.

When I compare the time spent in my own company in meetings with the time we spend praying about things, I am stunned. We are relatively prayerless.

A "bless us" here and a "lead us" there simply won't do. To run an excellent company, we need the wisdom of God, the ability to know what is the right thing to do at the right time in each situation (see Prov. 3:13–18). And lest we offer the excuse of being too busy, we should remember the words of Martin Luther, who, while in the midst of leading the Reformation, said, "I am so busy I must pray three hours a day."

Granted, not all companies are staffed with believers and open to prayer in meetings. I am blessed in my company with a team of disciples who relish time in prayer in order to discern God's will before planning and making decisions. This is not always the case—but in every case at least *you* can pray.

Meditate on the Word. The second discipline of running an excellent company is to immerse our minds in God's Word (see Phil. 4:8). If we have been entrusted with a company and the lives of those people affected in and by that company, it is required of us to spend more time (not less) thinking God's thoughts after him. A mere fifteen minutes a day won't cut it. We need to read, memorize, meditate, and apply God's truth in large doses.

I am not suggesting that as you read the Bible you will discover a passage that tells you how to do an acquisition. I am not one of those who believe that verses should jump out at you out of context in order to provide divine guidance. I am saying that the more we know of God's Word—the more our minds are filled with his truth—the more we will be able to discern God's answers and God's paths in the labyrinth of business decisions and strategies.

Learn constantly. One of the advantages of leading a business today is the wealth of great thought about business that is available to us. I have already listed some of my favorite authors, and I encourage you to read their books. As Christian business leaders, we should be reading everything we can get our hands on. Don't worry that the author isn't a Christian; read the book. Think over what you read. Look for the best ideas and practices. Just because a person isn't a follower of Christ doesn't mean that he or she can't be an expert in the field of sales or technology or continuous improvement.

However, reading isn't the same as learning. Learning happens when we confront data, reflect on that data, draw appropriate conclusions from that data, and make changes related to it. As my friend Peter Dickens says, "If there is no change, there is no learning." So when you read any book, take in the data. Turn it over in your mind. Think about it. Question it. Most important, apply your knowledge of Scripture to it to find consistency or inconsistency. Then, with a biblical grid overlaid, identify the implications and applications that are right for you. Just because the Bible doesn't use the term *Hedgehog Principle* (as does Jim Collins in *Good to Great*) doesn't mean that a kingdom business can't use it.

Interact with others. None of us is as smart as all of us. Gather together others who lead companies and who are questing after kingdom business. Meet to pray, to ask questions, to learn, to encourage one another, to hold one another accountable. Find the best practices in those around you and import them into your business as God leads you.

Don't limit your learning to other leaders. One of the best places for learning is from your employees. They work in the business every day and have lots of great ideas for making improvements that are just waiting for a hearing. Ask them what they think. Involve them in decision making and strategy. Admit you don't know it all, and you'll be amazed at the wisdom that will come to you. Don't forget—with every pair of hands you pay for, you also get a free brain. Use it!

Conclusion

There is no easy path to excellence in operations. The journey begins with a commitment to pursue excellence—ultimately for God's sake as well as for the blessing we will experience. Then, with the attitude of a continual learner, we can consider the ideas around us, taking what we choose and leaving the rest behind. There is much to be learned. Finally, with an idea that corresponds with our understanding of God's ways, we can make the changes that will enable us to lead the very best company we can, given the resources that God has put at our disposal.

10

ETHICS: LETTING
YOUR LIGHT SHINE

*I woke up thinking about an error on my tax return. I had
forgotten something—something that would cost me money.
Now that I remembered it (or more exactly now that God
had reminded me of it), I needed to redo my entire return.
Between the hassle of redoing my return and paying more
money, I was frustrated. Nevertheless, I knew the Lord had
brought this to my attention and that it was the right thing
to do.*

Enron. Tyco. Global Crossing. WorldCom. These companies were
once held to be synonymous with entrepreneurialism, leadership, innovation, and success. Today, they are signposts of corruption, scandal, dishonesty, fraud, and destruction. We can scarcely
open a newspaper without reading of another fall from grace in the
corporate world—Wall Street bankers cheating their investors, company executives taking huge bonuses while laying off workers, already-wealthy business owners committing insider trading. It seems that
American business is intent on validating the rest of the world's opinions about enterprise as inherently corrupt and corrupting.

On a more personal level we see the same thing. Just this morning I received an e-mail from a friend, a committed believer, who had discovered that his entire life's savings were gone because of a stock market scandal. I also remember well the day when a fellow believer in my church told me he would never do business with another Christian because he had been cheated so many times by his "brothers"! "At least," he said, "when I am cheated by non-Christians I am not disillusioned."

Several years ago a study was conducted comparing the marital satisfaction of professing Christians and non-Christians. Sadly, there was no difference. I fear that if a study were done of the ethical practices of Christian and non-Christian business professionals, the results would be similar. It is as if we have gotten swept up in the greed of our day and given in to the corruption with which we are surrounded—all the while professing to serve Christ in our businesses. How quickly we have forgotten the admonition of Solomon when he wrote, "Better a poor man whose walk is blameless than a rich man whose ways are perverse" (Prov. 28:6).

If we are to conduct our business in ways that truly honor Christ, if we view our company as an extension of our ministry to the Lord, and if we are to pursue the way of kingdom business, we must be committed to thinking and acting ethically, to knowing and doing what is right. This is a fundamental part of operational excellence—the fourth and final component of a kingdom business.

Defining Ethics

Years ago I was teaching a course on ethics to an Atlanta community leadership forum. As I was speaking, the U.S. Assistant District Attorney interrupted me. Tom said, "Mike, you need to emphasize that legal and ethical are not the same thing." His point was that something could be entirely legal—it could be within the bounds of the law—but still not be ethical; conversely, something could be ethical—morally right—but that action could land you in jail! I thought a great deal about the implication of Tom's words and realized that even today there is great confusion over the meaning of ethics.

Rather than bore you with a dictionary definition of ethics, I will ask you to think of the concept of ethics in its simplest terms. Ethics is nothing more complicated than knowing the difference between what is right and what is wrong and then acting accordingly. Ethics is about truth and falsehood. Ethics is about justice and injustice. Ethics is about what is proper and improper. Ethics is about making decisions. Ethics is, as politically incorrect as this may be, morality.

As human beings we are created in the image of God. God is moral, and we are moral. We know what is right and wrong, we are able to make choices consistent with our morality, and we experience the consequences of those choices. Ethics, then, is about knowing what is right, choosing what is right, and accepting responsibility for what we choose. This is part of what separates us from the animal kingdom. How odd that the world would seek to play down the place of morals, even questioning whether such a thing exists! How odd that we would seek to make business amoral, a place where ethics do not apply. To do so is to deny our very humanness! Here is yet another place the sacred-secular split impacts life; we often act as if ethics is for church, not for business.

Life is lived before our moral God. Life is lived before moral men and women. As Christians, we are called to live morally and ethically in this life, to do what is right. As Paul states, we live "taking pains to do what is right, not only in the eyes of the Lord but also in the eyes of men" (2 Cor. 8:21).

False Ethical Systems

Ethics is the stuff from which great philosophy flows. As people ponder the subject of right and wrong, they seek to categorize their thoughts into systems by which they may govern their lives. Those far more learned than I have written volumes on the subject. Yet even in my philosophical naïveté I must admit I am amazed at the ignorance (often willful) of those who write such books. It seems that the length to which some will go to create an ethical system that supports their lack of ethical behavior knows no limit. Let's take a look at some of the more popular yet false systems in play today.

Pragmatism. If it works, it's right. Do what you must to win, just don't get caught. Does that sound extreme? Is this philosophy limited to the world of Nazis and Communists? The truth is that those who make wealth, power, and prestige their god consistently apply this system to the decisions that they make. It is acceptable, for example, for a major international tobacco company to cheat growers in Central Asia by working through the government to fix prices at an artificially low rate. It is also acceptable for the same government to create a monopoly on tobacco production, keep the rates low, and reap huge profits by doing so. Why is it acceptable? Because it works. It provides product for the company and money for the government. It does not matter that the farmers are cheated and remain in abject poverty. It is pragmatism at its worst—a philosophical view that concepts or actions should be concerned with results, not the principles behind them.

And what about WorldCom? It was okay for the CEO to cheat thousands of employees and shareholders by taking questionable loans and guarantees from the company. His explanation and rationalization was that the board approved it. In other words, he justified his actions (which subsequently helped bring down a major company) because they achieved what he wanted and he could cover them with the thin veneer of "board approval." Ultimately, these actions (and others carried out at WorldCom) did not work. Nevertheless, the decisions were based on pragmatism, in that those involved believed they would work.

On a smaller scale, consider the builder who uses sub-specification materials or methods because it makes the project more profitable and the buyer can't tell the difference anyway. When the end justifies the means or clouds decisions as to what is right or wrong, that is pragmatism.

There is, of course, another problem with pragmatism. What constitutes "what works"? In business, the answer is often bound up with simply making more money, making the sale, making the deal. There is little or no thought given to the actual moral quality of the outcome.

Libertarianism. Libertarian thought says that what I do is neither right nor wrong as long as it doesn't hurt someone else. In this way drug use is legitimized, sexual perversion is accepted, and abortion is approved. How could cheating on taxes or falsifying an expense report be wrong as long as no person is affected? Libertarianism also denies the absolute nature of truth and morality and makes obvious damage the final judge of right and wrong.

Relativism. In relativism, there is no such thing as right and wrong but only what I personally feel is appropriate based on my sense of things. There is no standard, no truth—only that which I believe, and since it may not be what you believe, it applies only to me. It is all subjective. Everything is relative to my experience or my perception of your experience or to someone else's standards; it may be better or worse, but it is not right or wrong.

When I first encountered overt bribery in the former Soviet Union, I was shocked. Granted, up until that time I had lived in a bit of a bubble. Still, it was hard to grasp the openness with which government officials, taxi drivers, customs officers, and others extorted money from people. When I first began to challenge the practice, I was told that "it's the way it is here. It may not be that way in America, but it is here." In other words, right or wrong had more to do with geography than morality. That is a form of relativism.

Or look at Disney. Founded on the basis of family-friendly activities, television, and movies (can you remember the *Mickey Mouse Club* or *Flubber?*), the company has since acquired various studios, music companies, and other businesses that produce films with strong sexual and violent content hardly suitable for children. What is interesting to me is that Disney produces these movies under different brands to protect the original Disney image. In other words, it's not acceptable relative to the Disney name, but it's fully acceptable relative to another name owned by Disney. When things are right in one setting but wrong in another, that is a form of relativism.

No doubt there are many more false approaches to ethics that I haven't mentioned. These are the ones that I encounter the most in the business world—employed by those who deceive themselves into thinking they are ethical but who, in reality, are way off course.

A Biblical Approach to Ethics

So how does a Christian in business deal with ethics? The problem with false ethical systems is that they deny two fundamental realities: there is a God, and he has revealed in his Word what is right and what is wrong. As Christian thinker and apologist Francis Schaeffer put it (in his book by the same title), "He is there and he is not silent." And even when Scripture does not explicitly address a specific situation, the Bible contains principles that can be prayerfully applied in order to find the ethical path. Therefore, in pursuing biblical ethics, we have to wrap our thoughts around two key ideas: absolutism and applicational ethics.

Absolutism. In stark contrast to man-centered systems, absolutism maintains that there is an absolute and objective standard of what is right and wrong. Regardless of what appears to work, regardless of whether my action patently harms someone else, and regardless of what I think, there is a standard that is absolute, final, clear, and non-negotiable. The Bible clearly teaches absolutism. Beginning with the premise that God exists and is a moral being, the Bible teaches that God himself holds the knowledge of what is right and what is wrong. Moreover, Scripture proclaims that God has not kept this absolute standard a mystery to be discovered by accident and experience. On the contrary, he has clearly and consistently communicated his character, his standard, his commands, and his expectations to us in the form of propositional revelation (the words of the Bible). Therefore, to the Christian, the only option for an ethical system is what may be termed *biblical absolutism.*

In other words, as A.W. Tozer said many years ago in a pamphlet titled *How the Lord Leads,* "If the Bible says 'do it,' then do it; if it says 'don't do it,' then don't do it." It's that simple. Don't lie; tell the truth. Don't steal; be industrious. Don't be greedy; be generous. For much of life there is no doubt what the ethical path is because God has clearly told us how and where to walk.

Applicational ethics. But what about situations where the Bible is not explicit? While the Bible tells us to be kind, generous, and loving, it does not specifically tell me what to do about an employee who, for example, chooses to misuse the Family and Medical Leave Act to avoid correction or termination. Nor does Scripture tell me whether I should prosecute a shoplifter caught in my store or let him go with a warning. No Bible verse tells me when to give raises or how much they should be. How do I ensure ethical decisions and actions in cases like these?

The answer is that, as followers of Christ, we are constantly seeking to discover how God's unchangeable truth and morality as revealed in Scripture is to be applied to specific situations. This is what I term *applicational ethics.* Paul speaks of this in Ephesians 5:17: "Therefore do not be foolish, but understand what the Lord's will is." This is to be the bellwether for the kingdom professional: what does God say about this situation, and how do I apply what he says in obedience? With a thorough knowledge of Scripture, a growing knowledge of God's character, and prayerful dependence upon the Holy Spirit, I can discover the best and right path in any given circumstance.

Ethical Living in a Corrupt Society

In his letter to the Philippians, Paul describes the presence of Christians in the world in this way: "Do everything without complaining or arguing, so that you may become blameless and pure, children of God without fault in a crooked and depraved generation, in which you shine like stars in the universe as you hold out the word of life— in order that I may boast on the day of Christ that I did not run or labor for nothing" (Phil. 2:14–16). Paul's admonition is clear. Christians live in a dark world that is filled with corruption, sin, and unethical behavior. Their presence is to be in bold contrast to their surroundings. In place of darkness, they are light; in place of corruption, they are purity; in place of immorality, they are brilliant reflections of the moral character of God. In this way, Paul continues, we "hold out the word of life." Our behavior, by its very difference, is a testimony to the grace of God and serves to point people to Christ as the Savior of the world.

Nowhere does this have more potential impact than in the world of business. Where greed, selfishness, and ego have conspired to corrupt men and women, kingdom professionals highlight and even reprove unethical behavior as they carry out the absolute commands of Christ applied in and through their companies. They speak truth rather than lies (see Prov. 12:22). They apply fair balances and weights; that is, they deal fairly and honestly with customers (see Prov. 11:1; 16:11). They produce quality products and provide excellent service. They pay their taxes. Their word is their bond. They comply with laws and regulations. They make deals and stick with them even if the deals turn out to be less than desirable for them in the long run (see Ps. 15:4). They refuse to participate in bribery (see Deut. 16:19). They pay their debts (see Rom. 13:8).

Once, when America and the West were more closely aligned with our Judeo-Christian heritage, these practices were the norm. Today, the man or woman who consistently applies God's commands to business stands out as different, as light, as a kingdom professional.

Why It Matters

We could, in keeping with this topic, simply say that we do right because it's right. That would be true. However, Scripture reveals at least three critical reasons why it matters so much for business leaders to conduct themselves ethically.

First, ethical behavior provides testimony to our salvation and opens the door for an effective gospel witness. In my company, my associates and I have an enduring objective: to so live as to invite inquiry. What that means is that we want to walk with God and obey him in such a way that our colleagues and customers recognize that we are different—different to the point that they feel compelled to ask us the reason (see 1 Pet. 3:15). This does happen. Once, on a business trip while stuck in the Houston airport, one of my clients asked, "What is your passion in life? You are different, and I want to know why." Two hours later as we were boarding our flight, he even asked someone to change seats with him so he could sit next to me and finish hearing about Jesus and his power to transform lives!

Second, ethical business dealings protect our consciences before God. The author of Hebrews said, "Pray for us. We are sure that we have a clear conscience and desire to live honorably in every way" (Heb. 13:18). To seek to live, to lead a business, to enjoy life, to serve God, and all the other challenges we face daily is hard enough without the lead weight of a guilty conscience. Living God's way and conducting business according to his Word (while seeking forgiveness for the failures we will experience) is the only way to run the race.

Third, living morally in our companies prepares us for the judgment seat of Christ. Paul was greatly motivated by the reality that he would eventually give an account to God for the manner in which he lived his life: "For we must all appear before the judgment seat of Christ, that each one may receive what is due him for the things done while in the body, whether good or bad" (2 Cor. 5:10). Our dealings in business are not exempt from this ultimate evaluation by our Master.

Conclusion

I have not tried to solve ethical dilemmas in this chapter, nor have I tried to provide an ethical decision-making grid by which we can govern our lives. Rather, my purpose was simple. I wanted to make it clear that as Christian business leaders and as those seeking to build kingdom companies, we need to regard the matter of ethics as being of utmost importance. We are in desperate need of honest business-people. Our land groans under the weight of corruption at all levels of business and government. Greed and self-centeredness are carrying the day. God's answer is kingdom professionals placed in the midst of the darkness to shine as lights and, through their behavior, to demonstrate the reality of Christ's kingdom. May it ever be so.

MOVING TOWARD A
KINGDOM BUSINESS

11

THE INTEGRATION OF BUSINESS AS MISSION

Myron caught the vision and ran with it. After meeting him in Central Asia, I have watched as this owner of a food distribution company has stretched himself from a regional player in North America into an international trading company businessman with operations in Central Asia, North Africa, and Southeast Asia. Setting up food-processing operations among unreached people groups, Myron's for-profit business is a conduit for conveying the reality of the gospel as well as financial blessing in places of incredible need. Myron does not take time off from his work to do ministry. He has not set up a separate ministry supported by his company. Myron has discovered how to integrate his ministry and his business in a most profound way. That's why I say "Myron got it."

My company mission statement reminds me regularly that my business "exists to further the expansion of the kingdom of God among the unreached through the seamless integration of business as mission." While my colleagues and I have refined the wording of that statement over the years, the core purpose for which I started the company in 1998 (the expansion of God's kingdom among the unreached) has not changed, and the core strategy (the seamless integration of business as mission) has remained the same. It is this core strategy that I want to discuss in this chapter.

The Phases of Integration

As I have thought over this matter of integration (essentially ever since we started the company), and as I've observed other Christian business leaders seek to understand the relationship between their faith and their businesses, I have come to the conclusion that there are four distinct phases through which a business may pass on its journey. It is a kind of continuum between the two extremes of separation and seamless integration.

Separation. Sadly, far too many business leaders in America still operate at the "separation stage." They faithfully attend church on Sunday as well as other days of the week and are often involved in serving Christ in a traditional ministry format such as Sunday school or youth work, but the thought of bringing their faith into their professional lives seems either to never have crossed their minds or impossible.

I am not referring to the person who hypocritically worships God on Sunday and then lives for himself or herself the rest of the time. On the contrary, I am certain that the Christian business leaders I speak of are genuine disciples who long to know and please their Master. It is just that, beyond their personal morals, they simply don't see any connection between their Christianity and their business lives. Their businesses exist to provide them a living and enable them to give to the Lord's work, but their view of the Lord's work is centered on the church, and their ministry is not what they do at the office but only what they do when they are finally able to leave the office and "serve the Lord."

Perhaps this is due to the ever-present dualism, the separation between sacred and secular that pervades contemporary Christian culture. Perhaps they, like many in the world, still view business as a necessary evil. Perhaps they dream of being "freed from business" to "go into the ministry." Whatever the cause, the effect is still the same: their faith and their businesses exist in separation.

Invasion. There are others who have at least attempted to address the perceived gap between their faith and their business. While still viewing the business world as "of the world" and therefore basically evil (a misapplication of 1 John 2:15–17), they realize they are in it and are therefore committed to bringing Christ into the "darkness of business." These are the men and women who view the church as the center of light and business as the center of darkness; their mission, they conclude, is to foray from the church into business as a kind of evangelical raiding party. To integrate into the business community would be the same, in their minds, as Israel intermarrying with the heathen peoples they chased from the Promised Land, so rather than integrate, they invade.

To recognize one of these invaders, you have only to look for the fish on the business card, check out who's listed in the Christian Yellow Pages, or listen for the brother who inappropriately forces some Christianese language into business conversations. The invaders are alternately pugnacious and argumentative, proud of their victories over the godless business community when the rest of the invaders gather to exchange war stories, or discouraged over their lack of measurable impact or the last opportunity they squandered through cowardly silence.

In my experience, the ultimate problem with invaders is that their witness doesn't flow from the deep reality of their faith or from a healthy, biblical worldview. Instead, it is forced—a kind of contest they must endure because they are in business and not "in the ministry" which they think would most please God.

Overlay. Occasionally you will find the Christian business owner who, by virtue of position or force of personality, has the ability to overlay his or her faith on employees. I use the word *overlay* in the Old Testament word-picture sense—furniture of wood was overlaid with gold or silver, making it much more attractive. In the same way, the overlayer gilds the company with Christianity and, in doing so, considers it more attractive or beautiful.

Overlayers use Christian words, give generously from their profits, seek to treat employees well, and offer Bible studies and prayer meetings for workers. They hire corporate chaplains. They utilize symbols (like fish bumper stickers) and sincerely seek to bring Christ into their business. They are ethical and conduct their businesses in ethical ways. Overlayers often achieve their purpose: the "wooden" business is made more attractive by the "gold." These businesses are often incredibly nice places to work and a joy to customers—even winning awards for being different and better!

What, you ask, could be wrong with that? What is wrong about a person's wanting to have the gold of Christ overlay the wood of business? The problem is that to an overlayer, business is just that: wood. It may not be evil (in the way the invader views it), and thankfully it isn't to be ignored from a faith perspective (as the separator does), but it's still not something truly good in and of itself. It's neutral at best, and instead of seeking its transformation from the inside out for the kingdom, the overlayer seeks its beautification from the outside in. Nothing about the nature of business is ever truly addressed.

Seamless integration. Finally there is seamless integration. Integration means that multiple substances are joined together so that no future separation is possible. There are no parts, no compartments, and no boxes. There is integrity—oneness. That is how kingdom professionals view and approach business; indeed, this is how they live their entire lives. Every aspect of their lives—home, church, leisure, and business—is under the rule of God. They see everything as part of God's kingdom and subject to God's reign. They don't leave God in the closet when they finish personal devotions. They walk with God from the closet to the breakfast table, and then from the breakfast table to the office, sales call, or factory. They are no closer to God in church than in the workplace. There is no difference between doing a deal and serving communion. Life is a whole and is holistically submitted to God's authority. Wherever they are and whatever they are doing, they are serving and worshiping the Master. There is no sacred and secular, no dichotomy. There is no business and ministry. All is sacred. All is ministry. And because they think this way, they are free to honor God joyfully anywhere they may be.

Now, to the business leader who views life this way, business and faith could never be separate; nor would this business leader identify an area of life as darkness to be invaded for God or something plain needing to be beautified by external adornment. Since this leader views business as part of God's call, he or she ministers in it, from it, and through it. Business is not the totality of ministry any more than it is the totality of life. It is a venue for service, just as family, church, and community are. God is at the center, integrating everything and flowing into and through every avenue of life.

On the Path to Seamless Integration

My coworkers and I are all too aware of our shortcomings and failures in our own journey toward seamless integration. But we are on the way. We can serve as an encouragement to others who are on the journey with us and to those Christian business owners contemplating what the journey might mean if they decide to take it.

What does seeking seamless integration look like in my company? In the preface I outlined our nonprofit involvement in providing economic traction to persecuted minority Christians who live among predominantly Muslim, Hindu, or Buddhist peoples. Our U.S.-based, for-profit operations are also built on this kind of kingdom impact model; as one of the premier small-business consulting firms in the country, we bring growth strategies and processes to our clients that often produce spectacular results. Yet we view this as every bit the ministry that our work overseas is. How is that possible?

First, we seek to work for our clients wholeheartedly as unto the Lord (see Eph. 6:5–7) and to view all of our labor as an offering to Christ. Second, we spend much time in prayer for our clients and our kingdom impact among them. Third, we encourage one another to, as our values put it, "live lives that invite inquiry." Fourth, we seek to provide ministry to everyone with whom we work, depending upon where they are in their spiritual journey. To our unbelieving clients we seek to exhibit the integrity and character of Christ and to take every opportunity he provides to share God's truth with them. To our believing clients we constantly encourage them to live for Christ, and sometimes we involve them in the sacrificial service opportunity of our foreign work. Finally, we seek to operate according to the principles of excellence and ethics discussed earlier. In these ways, we are always seeking to move farther down the path to the seamless integration of business as mission.

Conclusion

So where are you? Where is your life, your business on the continuum? The point is not to be finished. The point is to be on the journey and moving toward the destination. I, for one, am not done. I am still learning, growing, changing, and correcting.

12

ACTION PLANNING FOR KINGDOM BUSINESS

Deborah came to me to discuss how she could turn her engineering firm into an effective kingdom company. Her heart for God was evident. Her passion for missions was clear. Her desire to see her U.S. employees blessed while reaching out to the lost in other countries was as strong as I'd seen anywhere.

So what do we actually do with all of this? How do we actually take the practical steps of turning this intention into action? How do you and I move our companies further into God's plan and realize the power of kingdom business?

The answers that I suggest are twofold. First, we must radically change the way we think: we must reorder our mental categories and our life priorities to reflect biblical truth. And second, we must have and follow a strategic plan that moves us closer to our goal.

Changing the Way We Think

One of my seminary professors, Howard Hendricks, used to say that Christians have a problem called "hardening of the categories." What he meant was that it is our tendency to get locked into patterns of thinking that keep us from seeing what God is doing in the world and what he would have us do. Another way of saying this is that our perceptions are governed by our beliefs, and our beliefs are not always biblical.

The sacred-secular split is one example of "hardening of the categories," as is the belief in a strict separation between clergy and laity. Other categories of thought that blind us to God's constant innovation include the ideas that missions is done by missionaries, that businesspeople are supposed to give rather than go, and that the core of Christianity is only about the individual salvation of men and women and has little to do with society as a whole.

What I find interesting about this is the parallel between the things we hold dear that keep us from understanding and doing the will of God and the traditions that blinded religious people in Jesus' day. Look at the encounter Jesus had with the Pharisees following their criticism of his disciples' eating with unwashed hands.

> He [Jesus] replied, "Isaiah was right when he prophesied about you hypocrites; as it is written:
> 'These people honor me with their lips,
>   but their hearts are far from me.
> They worship me in vain;
>   their teachings are but rules taught by men.'
> You have let go of the commands of God and are holding on to the traditions of men."
>
> And he said to them: "You have a fine way of setting aside the commands of God in order to observe your own traditions!... Thus you nullify the word of God by your tradition that you have handed down. And you do many things like that." (Mark 7:6–13)

The problem with the Pharisees, according to Jesus, was that they had allowed handed-down traditions to become more important than the truth of God's Word. The effect of this was to nullify or void its meaning. The same thing occurs today when we accept a tradition or traditional way of thinking that blinds us to what God is really saying in Scripture.

The hard part about all of this is that it is extremely difficult to see where we have been blinded by tradition. After all, it is our way and the way we've always done it. It's accepted. It must be right. And since everyone else seems to be doing it this way, there is no real pressure to change. Indeed, if we do see something different, we often reject it because we think, "Everyone else can't be wrong!"

Even if we do begin to see things a bit differently and to realize that perhaps this is what God is saying, it is easier to ignore what we are beginning to perceive than to embrace it, for the simple reason that change is difficult. Years ago, my family and I lived in rural Texas, and our house was on a dirt road—unless it rained. When it rained, the dirt turned into a thick mud known as "black gumbo." Driving through the mud would create deep ruts that, when the sun came out, hardened into semipermanent ruts, often eight inches deep. If your tire got into one of these hardened ruts, you were going to go where the rut led—whether you wanted to or not. You could practically take your hands off the wheel and let the car follow the rut to its destination. In fact, the only way to break free of that rut was with a violent jerk of the steering wheel. I think that's what it takes to break us out of our mental ruts as well. Even though we may perceive gradually, God often has to jerk us out of our traditions in order to get us to act on his truth and will for our lives.

So, if we are to have a kingdom business, we must change the way we think, or, more likely, we must have a jolt from God to change the way we think, to shake up our categories, and to challenge our traditional understanding of his plan for business.

For me, this jolt took place when I first traveled to the former Soviet Union, as I described in the preface. Seeing the enormous needs of this newly independent Muslim part of the world and the staggeringly positive response to business conversations, I was challenged to the core of my being to rethink my personal ministry. My first reaction was to fit my experience into my existing categories or paradigm: if God was calling me to be involved in this part of the world, it must mean that I should leave my business and become a missionary. However, God clearly shut the door to this and forced me, literally, to reexamine my approach. I knew I was called to this area of the world; I also knew I was *not* called to change careers. Finally, I was led by the Holy Spirit to understand that a new way, at least new to me, was opening: business *as* mission as opposed to choosing between business *and* mission.

One of the major motivations for my writing this book has been to throw out a challenge to the conventional way that we, as Christians, think about business, about ministry, and about missions. I am convinced that as we begin to think more biblically about God's calling to business and his purpose for it, we will be able to participate more fully in what he is doing at home and around the world.

Planning the Way We Work

Thinking differently leads to acting differently. If we begin to realize that God has sanctified business and called us into it while inviting us to be involved with him in his global work, we will feel a powerful impetus to change how we live and how we lead our businesses. We will want to build kingdom businesses. But how do we actually do that? How do we turn our thoughts into reality? The answer is with a kingdom business plan (and a lot of prayer). This section will outline the steps required in thinking through, formulating, and implementing such a plan.

Create a kingdom foundation. All solid business or strategic plans are built on a strong foundation of values, ideology, and beliefs. Therefore, the first step in creating your kingdom business plan is to formulate your thoughts about kingdom business in general. Do you believe in it? Do you believe you are called into business? What are the values that will govern your business? What principles will guide its operational decisions? These are the ingredients of a solid foundation.

Specifically, I would recommend taking the following categories and writing out what you believe about each of them: profit, people, growth, service or quality, productivity, and innovation. These are a starting point. You may add to or subtract from the list. The point is to express your heartfelt beliefs about the key components of business and to base these components on your growing understanding of kingdom business. For example, my company has worked out specific values over the years. To articulate the guiding principles upon which our company is built, we set forth the following corporate values:

- We will always seek mutually beneficial outcomes in all that we do—for our clients, our associates, and our vendors and for any people with whom we labor.
- We will operate in a fiscally responsible manner.
- We will seek continual learning and improvement so that what is done is done well and with full commitment.
- We will live lives that invite inquiry.
- We will maintain the priorities of family and friendship.
- We will endeavor to find maximum enjoyment in whatever we do.

You will notice that I haven't attached Bible verses or included religious language in these values. There is a reason for this. I am seeking to integrate biblical truth, not just import biblical words, into business. This forces me to think harder and more thoroughly about my corporate values.

Articulate a kingdom direction. The foundation of biblical truth and kingdom thinking leads to the formulation of a kingdom direction. I use three different categories to express this.

Vision. Vision is a broad, expansive statement of the general direction in which your company is going. It is the extension of your current beliefs into a distant future. On a very practical level, I encourage people to ask and answer this question: "What would my company look like if all my values were lived to a 'Level 10,' that is, fully realized?" The answer is your vision. For my company, our kingdom vision statement reads: To partner with God in establishing a worldwide, self-sustaining, reproducing network of kingdom businesses.

Mission. Mission is a narrower definition of your vision. Some would say it is your vision with metrics. In my usage, the term *mission statement* is simply a tighter definition of why my company exists: seamless integration of business and ministry for the expansion of God's kingdom among the unreached.

Purpose. A kingdom purpose statement is the expression of what you believe God has as his specific will for your company. It is how you state your understanding of the intersection between your business and God's kingdom activities. Again, here is ours: provision, i.e., to create and grow an economic engine that

- provides for the needs of our families,
- provides opportunities for discipleship with our clients, and
- provides for the financial needs of the Overseas Business Development Project.

Each of these three statements expresses a nuance of my understanding of God's plan for my company. There is a vision of what will be someday. There is a more specific sense of mission or intent. There is a blunt reason or purpose that the company exists. It took years to arrive at these statements in their present form; they are constantly being reexamined. As you begin working on yours, don't be discouraged if they don't feel like a finished product; they most likely are not.

Identify kingdom targets and objectives. The foundational and philosophical portion of the plan is complete in values, vision, mission, and purpose. Now you must turn your philosophy into strategy and your intention into action. To do this, you identify and write down kingdom targets and objectives. Since the kingdom business plan is an integrated plan, blending your business and kingdom aspirations and your targets and objectives will reflect this.

A *target*, as I use the term, refers to a three-year goal for your business. An *objective* means a one-year goal. Consequently, you will write goals (measurable and realistic) for the key aspects of your business, such as revenues, expansion, staffing, profitability, ministry, and missions.

Consider the example on the following table:

Targets and objectives

Critical Success Area	One-Year Objectives	Three-Year Targets
Projects Growth	25 overseas projects running Exit from 2 $390k for project funding	30 overseas projects running Exit from 6 $600k for project funding
Financial Performance	$1.6 million in revenue	$2.8 million in revenue
Client Service	80% approval rate on client surveys	80% approval rate on client surveys
Practice Expansion	Add 1 affiliate	Add 1 affiliate

Notice in the targets and objectives that the overseas work, which is the core purpose of the company, is listed first and is blended with simple business targets and objectives. In my mind, the achievement of one without the other is both philosophically impossible and financially untenable.

Focus on a few pivotal strategies. A pivotal strategy is a major activity—a long-term project, a big initiative—that spans many months and sometimes even the course of a year. It is, as opposed to an action item, an activity that will greatly impact the achievement of the targets and objectives you have set in your plan. Try to limit these to three to five; too many, and your plan will become unwieldy. Here are mine:

- Execute marketing/business development plan
- Document/improve all overseas project processes into SOP manual.
- Recruit and launch two strong affiliates.

- Increase number of strong overseas project leaders to sixteen; project staff to two.
- Expand board of directors to reflect long-term expansion plans.
- Hold monthly management team prayer sessions.

My business is fairly simple. Therefore, the pivotal strategies are also simple. Nevertheless, in implementing each of the strategies over the course of a year, the movement toward a more fully blended kingdom business, as well as greater achievement of our kingdom purpose, is taking place.

Draft and assign quarterly action items. What turns a plan into reality is action. Break your plan down into a list of ten or fewer action items that will help you implement your pivotal strategies and achieve your kingdom targets and objectives. Limit these to what can be achieved over the next quarter. Make sure the action item is assigned to someone on your team. Remember, "Any job that is everybody's job is actually nobody's job." My plan follows:

Item	Action	Who	Status
1	Create consistent reporting format/schedule for project	Tim	
2	Get current MO Send and confirm with all in-country partners	Tim	
3	Set project calendar and determine leadership resource allocation	Tim	
4	Complete Phase 1 curriculum revision	Tim Mike	Done

5	Issue client survey and summarize results	Gary	
6	Execute professional services marketing/BD plan	Gary	
7	Plan midyear client event	Mike	

Schedule regular accountability. Accountability is the key to making all this happen. I recommend three forms of accountability for your kingdom business plan. First, hold a monthly meeting or conference call with all of the people involved in the plan to check the status of action items; this is a chance for anyone who is stuck to ask for help. Second, update the action items every quarter. Review the objectives and targets as well as the pivotal strategies, then create a new list of action items for the next quarter. Third, seek an outside coach or partner, perhaps another kingdom business owner, with whom you can meet to pray and provide updates on your progress.

It has been said by someone (and repeated by many) that people don't plan to fail, they fail to plan. In the same way, you and I can have all the desire in the world to have a kingdom business, but until we create a plan and execute that plan, it will not happen.

Conclusion

The gap between our current reality and what God desires is bridged in two ways. We must think differently—we must change the way we think and adopt biblical principles and attitudes. And we must act differently—we must plan and implement our plan to achieve our new direction.

EPILOGUE

The purpose of this book is simple. The book is not meant to answer all of the questions that a kingdom professional will face; the field is too new to even ask all the questions, much less answer them. Instead, I am hoping to challenge Christian business leaders to think and to pray—to seek God and to have fellowship with other believers—about the enormous potential within business to impact society for Christ and his kingdom.

We are living in the Business Age. Many Christian and secular historians would agree that the historic role of nation-states is rapidly passing from the scene and is being replaced by the corporation. Companies, and not countries, will have the greatest impact in our world in the future. Shouldn't the Christian business community see this as a great opportunity? Shouldn't we seek to capitalize on the doors that are open before us? Shouldn't we view this as the ultimate chance for business to play a role in societal transformation and in the spread of the gospel?

To do so requires that we think differently about God, about his kingdom, about his purposes in the world, and about business. My goal has been to outline conclusions I have drawn from decades of biblical study and from seeking, in my own life, to establish a king-dom company—a company that is based on clear scriptural teaching and aligned with God's clear scriptural purposes. I hope that as you have read these pages you have followed along with me in my jour-ney and that each of you will take seriously the challenge of kingdom business and truly become a kingdom professional. If this happens, you will be writing the next chapters.

APPENDIX: RECOMMENDED RESOURCES FOR THE KINGDOM PROFESSIONAL

Books

Beckett, John D. *Loving Monday: Succeeding in Business Without Selling Your Soul.* Downers Grove, Ill.: InterVarsity, 2001.

Burkett, Larry. *Business by the Book: The Complete Guide of Biblical Principles for the Workplace.* Nashville, Tenn.: Thomas Nelson, 1998.

Collins, Jim. *Good to Great: Why Some Companies Make the Leap... and Others Don't.* New York: HarperCollins, 2001.

Collins, Jim, and Jerry Porras. *Built to Last: Successful Habits of Visionary Companies.* New York: HarperCollins, 2002.

Guiness, Os. *The Call: Finding and Fulfilling the Central Purpose of Your Life.* Nashville, Tenn.: W Publishing Group, 2003.

Rundle, Steve, and Tom Steffen. *Great Commission Companies: The Emerging Role of Business in Missions.* Downers Grove, Ill.: InterVarsity, 2003.

Silvoso, Ed. *Anointed for Business.* Ventura, Calif.: Regal, 2002.

Yamamori, Tetsunao, and Kenneth A. Eldred, eds. *On Kingdom Business: Transforming Business Through Entrepreneurial Strategies.* Wheaton, Ill.: Crossway, 2003.

Web Site

Kingdom Business Forum, www.kingdombusinessforum.org

ABOUT THE AUTHOR

Michael R. Baer has worked in the field of organizational and leadership development for over twenty-five years. He has founded several businesses, including the business advisory and strategic consulting firm that is his current company, a construction and remodeling business, and a bed and breakfast inn. In addition, as executive director of an international mission organization specializing in microenterprise, Mike has launched a small business incubation process used in over seventeen countries.

As a leader in small business growth practices, Mike has experience in a variety of industries, including staffing, manufacturing, high tech, media, education, healthcare, construction and development, federal and local government, education, engineering, and financial services. Mike has served as a coach to clients in the United States, Canada, Europe, China, and several former republics of the Soviet Union, providing support in strategic planning, leadership development, change mastery, total quality management, management coaching, acquisition management, business planning and finance, small business incubation, sales systems, customer service, and turnaround endeavors.

Prior to his work in business, Mike was in pastoral ministry for fifteen years. He holds a ThM from Dallas Theological Seminary.